What commentators are saying about *Nation in Transit*

'Today's politics is dominated by negative campaigning which is fuelling misery and pessimism. Phil Anderson has set out a programme to challenge that and reminds us that in politics we must enthuse and inspire, not just condemn.'

JACKIE DOYLE-PRICE MP

'Phil Anderson has taken his intelligent, compassionate, and community-focused style of politics and applied it to some of the biggest issues facing Britain today. Our political debate needs to include more voices like this.'

STEPHEN METCALFE MP

'The decision to leave the EU exposed deep levels of discontent in the UK. *Nation in Transit* provides a helpful and hopeful analysis for where we go now. As we search for ideas to address the issues that Brexit exposed, Phil Anderson has focused his political knowledge and experience in a way that suggests a new direction. I hope we pay attention to this timely and important publication.'

DR DAVID LANDRUM

'This isn't a book that simply diagnoses the issues facing us: it offers a broad range of radical ideas for treating the underlying problems, rather than the "more of the same" approach that characterises current political engagement. None of these issues are simple, and none will be solved easily, but *Nation in Transit* – with its chapters on subjects from the allocation of social housing to the way we create and administer money – opens a discussion we need to hold publicly, and as soon as possible.'

DR GUY BRANDON

NATION IN TRANSIT

NATION IN TRANSIT

A manifesto for post-Brexit Britain

Phil Anderson

Muddy
Pearl

First published in 2016 by
Muddy Pearl, Edinburgh, Scotland.

www.muddypearl.com
books@muddypearl.com

British Library Cataloguing in Publication Data
A catalogue record for this book is available from the British Library

ISBN 978 1 910012 41 3

Typeset by Waverley Typesetters
Printed and bound in Great Britain by Bell & Bain Ltd, Glasgow

CONTENTS

INTRODUCTION: BREXIT GROUND ZERO

Living where I do, you become a connoisseur of white vans. Big ones with ply lining, tool racks, and enough space to lug everything you need for a small building site. Medium-sized ones which act as workshop, stock room, mobile office, and canteen for thousands of plumbers, carpenters, and electricians. And small ones which you can use like a car but still claim tax breaks because they are treated as a business expense.

You become pretty familiar with white van accessories too. The big ones normally have a collection of dents where they got too close to a forklift and an industrial grade padlock on the back to stop anyone nicking the owner's gear. Small ones get fluffy dice and alloy wheels. And the medium-sized ones invariably have a sticker saying 'no tools kept in this van overnight' and some scrawled writing in the dirt on the back suggesting that the vehicle is 'also available in white'.

White Van Man is the salt of the earth and the soul of the nation. He (or occasionally she) works hard, plays hard, looks after his family, and takes pride in his home. He's nobody's fool, despite what the broadsheets think of him. He never goes on strike, rarely throws a sickie, but will walk off the job rather than be talked down to or short changed. When he thrives, Britain thrives, and when he doesn't it is a warning sign that the nation had better sit up and take notice.

Right now, White Van Man isn't thriving. The most recent accessory to appear on Thurrock's white van fleet was a 'Vote

Leave' sticker, and it didn't reflect a new-found interest in European politics. White Van Man has never really been a political animal. He will admit to admiring Maggie Thatcher, but that's about it. That sticker was never about policies, it was an expression of frustration, disillusionment, anger, and a deep sense that things aren't right and no-one is admitting to the problem, let alone solving it.

It therefore came as no surprise that Thurrock and its South Essex neighbours registered one of the highest 'Leave' votes in the country, with over 70% of voters demanding that we quit the EU and 'take our country back'. Essex didn't sleepwalk into Brexit; it kicked open the door and angrily demanded that Britain leave now before there was any trouble. If the referendum was a political earthquake then this was the epicentre; the 'ground zero' from which the political order has been shaken to the core and from where the future shape of the nation will be determined.

That future shape is what we now need to figure out. Most people are smart enough to realise that simply leaving the EU won't solve all of their problems. They just knew that something had to change, and this was the biggest opportunity for change that they had been offered in a generation. Voters on both sides of the referendum debate are now looking for a clear, positive vision for a post-Brexit Britain that can unite the nation and offer a course through the risks and opportunities that lie ahead.

This book is not about the post-Brexit angst being suffered by 'Remain' voters coming to terms with a future outside of the EU that they never really thought would happen. It is about the pre-Brexit unhappiness and disaffection that led so many people to vote against a political system that they no longer trusted or believed in. And because of that, it doesn't focus primarily on the international treaties or trade deals that have to be negotiated as we put this most controversial of democratic decisions into effect.

Instead it offers practical solutions to the underlying problems that led to Britain's Brexit blues in the first place. Ending the waste of human potential that is mass unemployment and the scandal of low-wage poverty. Getting people out of broken, dysfunctional council estates. Fixing the inequities of the finance system and enabling more people to know the security of owning their own home. Sensibly balancing immigration with an open, globally connected society. Re-establishing thriving communities founded on strong and deep relationships. Funding public investment, giving a bigger role to charity and community groups, and stewarding the natural and built environments for future generations. The answers combine radical political courage with grass roots Essex reality; because if the solutions don't work for White Van Man then they probably won't work at all.

This book is for all of my friends, neighbours, and relatives who have ever got behind the wheel of a white van. And given that not all of them are big readers, it's also for the decision-makers who make the promises and implement the policies that affect their lives. Some of those decision-makers are my friends too and, just like White Van Man, they're not nearly as bad as the papers would have you believe.

1

END THE MISERY

We hold these truths to be self-evident, that all men are created equal, that they are endowed by their Creator with certain unalienable rights, that among these are life, liberty and the pursuit of happiness.

THOMAS JEFFERSON

Money can't buy you happiness but it does bring you a more pleasant form of misery.

SPIKE MILLIGAN

My neighbours are the most miserable people in Britain. You don't just have to take my word for it; it has been proved by official research. On 24 July 2012, Britain's Office for National Statistics published its first comprehensive national survey of wellbeing.[1] One of the sections was a regional breakdown, which gave the results for every local authority area in the UK. My own borough of Thurrock in Essex had come bottom of the list for life satisfaction.[2] As expected, the following morning the national press descended and ran a series of articles branding our home town 'the country's capital of misery'. Some of those they interviewed were even less complimentary. One resident described our area as 'one big cesspit', while others felt it was 'in need of a facelift' and somewhere they only lived 'because I have to'.

Just a couple of decades ago, Essex Man was held up as an icon of British optimism; the embodiment of a future filled with opportunity. So why hasn't it worked out that way?

My neighbours are unhappy because some of them are unemployed, and even if they aren't their children either can't find work at all or can't get the kind of secure, moderately well-paid jobs which the rest of society seems to expect and which they themselves once took for granted.

They are unhappy because too many of them live on grotty, run-down council estates in badly built, poorly maintained houses. When they walk out of their front doors they experience a gloomy environment marred by litter, vandalism, and the nagging fear of crime. Those who can afford to buy their own home are unhappy because they face years of saving for a deposit followed by three decades of crippling mortgage and interest payments before they pay it off.

They are unhappy because almost half of them have grown up without knowing the security that comes from living in a stable two-parent family. They are confused about their own relationships, lack decent role models to learn from, and have discovered from bitter personal experience the pain that family breakdown causes to both adults and children.

My white neighbours are unhappy because they believe that immigrants are moving in to take away 'their' jobs, 'their' houses, and 'their' public services. My black neighbours are unhappy because they worry that they will be discriminated against in the workplace and that their children cannot walk the streets in safety without fear of being attacked by racist gangs.

My older neighbours are unhappy because they seem to remember a time when everyone in their street knew each other by name, everyone was a member of a local club or society, and everyone was willing to spare the time to look out for each other, and that doesn't seem to happen anymore.

And pretty much everyone is unhappy because they are constantly being told that the world is heating up, rainforests are disappearing, the ice caps are melting, polar bears are dying, and they feel powerless to do anything about it.

This sense of unease and dissatisfaction which so visibly affects Thurrock is repeated to varying degrees across the rest of Britain, and in fact across the whole of the western world. Most of the problems which afflicted previous generations are simply no longer an issue for people today. We enjoy levels of security and prosperity which our own ancestors could only dream of. But it has not made us happy and it has not convinced us that our society is entering the twenty-first century asking the right questions, let alone offering us the right answers.

I'm a Brexiter, get me out of here

When people feel that unhappy, human nature says that they will eventually start looking for someone to blame. The list has been growing steadily for a decade: politicians, bankers, bureaucrats, fat cats, and, especially, immigrants.

Anyone involved in local politics in Thurrock has seen this pattern emerging for a while. As long ago as 2007, the BNP (a far-right anti-immigrant party) was polling up to 25% of the vote in local elections in Thurrock. They largely faded from the scene after the 2010 general election. Their decline was mirrored by the rise of UKIP, whose slightly more nuanced anti-immigration and anti-establishment message allowed them to attract disaffected right-wing Conservatives and angry white working-class Labour voters who wanted a means to vent their frustration but would not have been willing to go quite as far as supporting the BNP. The three voter groups combined proved a winning combination in local elections, leading to a run of UKIP council victories. By the 2015 general election Jackie Doyle-Price MP knew she had a fight on her hands to hold Thurrock.

At the start of the campaign Labour and the Conservatives were neck and neck in the polls, with UKIP only a few points behind. It seemed clear that whoever lost the most votes to UKIP was also going to lose the election. As the weeks flew by and the polls tightened, UKIP steadily gained ground, turning an already close two-way battle into a true three-way fight to the finish. The pundits and the bookies started to point to Thurrock as UKIP's best chance of general election gain, and with that prediction came intense media scrutiny and an increasingly aggressive political atmosphere. When I arrived at the count after a long day of door knocking and telephoning, I could tell straight away that the result in Thurrock was going to be national news. No less than three satellite vans were parked up outside, and in the foyer you could hardly move for TV and radio crews looking for someone to interview. Votes were counted, then re-counted. A secretive commotion took place between the Returning Officer and the Election Agents (which we later discovered was the result of several hundred Conservative ballots being found in the Labour pile). My lasting memory of that election night was the roar from the crowd of activists as it was announced that Jackie had successfully fought off all comers and held the seat.

However, if anyone though that 2015 was the high-water mark of anti-establishment anger, they were to be proved wrong in the most dramatic way possible. With a Conservative majority government in place, the promised in/out referendum on Britain's membership of the EU was called for June 2016. Unlike a 'normal' election campaign where local activists have a pretty good insight into the mood on the ground, we had no real idea which way the vote was going. We knew Thurrock and Essex would probably vote to leave, but what was happening in the rest of the country? The polls said it was becoming too close to call, but then the polls had got it wrong in 2015, so could they be trusted?

The shock on Friday morning when it became clear that the UK had actually voted to leave the EU was simply unprecedented. Within less than 24 hours the pound had crashed, global stock markets had wobbled, the Prime Minister had resigned, and the leader of the opposition was facing a vote of no confidence. Britain was entering unknown political territory. The campaigns had (inevitably) focused on the relative merits of EU membership, not on the detail of what would happen if we actually voted to leave. Now we were rushing headlong into a vacuum of leadership and vision with no clear plan for what Britain outside the EU could or should look like.

As the result sank in and the post-referendum analysis began, the sheer scale of the anti-EU vote in Thurrock started to become clear. The highest 'Leave' percentage in the UK had been in the small rural districts of Boston and South Holland, which were unique in having large and rapidly growing immigrant populations of Eastern European agricultural workers. This was predictable and in some ways understandable, but hardly representative of the country at large. The second-highest 'Leave' vote in the country was in Thurrock and neighbouring Castle Point. Over 72% of the population in both areas had voted to leave the EU. Now we were not just 'the country's capital of misery', we were also 'Britain's most Eurosceptic area'. Disaffection and anger had turned into rejection of an entire political system.

Angry of South Essex

For those not familiar with Essex geography, Thurrock sits on the north bank of the Thames estuary, 20 miles east of London. The landscape is a mixture of semi-rural and post-industrial, with the remains of factories, refineries, and power stations still littering the river front. The area today is best known for retail and logistics, being dominated by the M25 motorway, the Dartford river crossings, the ports and warehouses, and the massive Lakeside shopping centre.

Throughout its history, Thurrock has been an industrious place where people came to seek opportunities and make a life for themselves. The Romans established salt workings on the river marshes, and the Anglo-Saxons dug for iron ore at Orsett. Medieval villagers grazed sheep and farmed the land. Sand, gravel, and chalk were dug out to help build the growing London metropolis, and increasingly its rubbish got dumped back into the abandoned workings. The Victorians built forts to defend the river and opened a deep-water harbour for their new-fangled steamships at Tilbury. In the mid-twentieth century the availability of open land with good river access led to the construction of massive oil refineries, cement works, and power stations. At the same time the population was growing enormously, with Thurrock's sleepy towns and villages in some cases tripling in size as new estates were erected to house workers moving in from the bombed-out terraces of east London.

Although mostly given to hard graft and getting on with life, the citizens of Thurrock have been no strangers to events which have shaped our national history. In 1381, the village of Fobbing became the initial flashpoint of the peasants' revolt after King Richard II's botched attempts to impose a poll tax. Within weeks, Wat Tyler was leading the men of Essex and Kent to march on London, and Lollard priest John Ball was preaching his radical egalitarian sermon 'when Adam delved and Eve span, who was then the gentleman?' Even today local mums push their buggies around Wat Tyler Park, mostly oblivious to the area's revolutionary history. In 1588, Queen Elizabeth I came to Tilbury to address her troops on the eve of the Spanish Armada. In a masterpiece of politically incorrect oratory she assured her subjects that 'I know I have the body but of a weak and feeble woman; but I have the heart and stomach of a king, and of a king of England too'. The Armada was duly defeated and England saved from invasion, an event commemorated by a couple of beacons along the river and a profusion of names like Drake Road and Galleon Road on the Chafford Hundred housing estate.

Modern Thurrock is, by most measures, a typical English borough. We have average incomes, average employment prospects, average health, and even the weather is slightly better than Britain's rather rainy norms. We do not experience the extremes of poverty and oppressive rulers which led the men of Fobbing to march behind Wat Tyler, nor do we face the threat of war and invasion which caused the army to rally for Queen and Country at Tilbury. But something is not right in the land of revolting peasants and feisty queens. Somehow the description 'the unhappiest place in England' and the massive vote to leave the EU didn't take people by surprise. Thurrock at the dawn of the twenty-first century has a swirling undercurrent of discontent, frustration, and anger, and that was showing up clearly in the statistics.

What happens when the giants are dead

Discontent and anger left to fester are bad for a nation and bad for democracy. They cause people to follow a well-worn path that leads initially to cynicism and disengagement, then ultimately into the arms of populists or dictators. Both offer easy and superficially attractive answers, based on a recipe of 'tell people whatever they want to hear' and 'find someone else to blame' with a big helping of so-called 'strong leadership' to steamroller over the inevitable flaws and inconsistencies. By the time it gets to this stage, more moderate voices find it incredibly difficult to compete. Realism lacks the rhetorical appeal of fantasy, and a willingness to make difficult compromises can all too easily be caricatured as hypocrisy. The unhappiness which is revealing itself in Thurrock and across Britain has to be addressed urgently and directly, because the longer it is left to fester the more likely it is to be stirred up and exploited by those who would use it for their own purposes.

What does it take to make people happy? How can human beings live a life that flourishes in every way; materially, emotionally, relationally and spiritually? This question has exercised poets, theologians, artists, and philosophers for thousands of years. But until recently it has rarely been given much thought by practical politicians. The reason is probably that, up to a point, the answers are obvious. When William Beveridge wrote his famous report which led to the creation of the modern British welfare state, he identified 'five giants' of squalor, ignorance, want, idleness, and disease which needed to be overcome. No-one is likely to overlook a giant. Big, obvious social problems demand big, obvious solutions, and you don't need clever research to work out whether people would be happier free from disease and hunger.

That point of obviousness has now been passed in much of the developed world. We have the most productive economies the earth has ever seen, but millions are unemployed. We have comprehensive healthcare systems, but health and life expectancy still vary massively. We have free education for all, but young people still enter adult life lacking basic literacy. Beveridge's welfare-state reforms enjoyed broad political support and the backing of the vast majority of the public. Solving today's social problems is far more contentious. It is by no means clear whether more of yesterday's solutions will help the situation, or will actually make matters worse.

In some cases we are no longer even sure what the problem is any more. Poverty is easy to define when people lack food, clean water, and shelter. What we call poverty in modern western societies represents riches beyond the dreams of our recent ancestors and our global neighbours. Yet it still looks and feels like poverty. And for every voice saying that we need to provide more for those who have less, there is another suggesting that to live sustainably we all need to consume less and that increasing material wealth is no solution at all.

How do you promote wellbeing when you are past the point of obviousness? In democracies there is a compelling reason for practical politicians to join with the theologians and philosophers in looking for answers. If people believe that your policies and leadership will further their wellbeing, they are more likely to vote for you. Voters may not always be right about what is best for themselves or society, but they aren't stupid and they do have the final say. So if you really want to know whether your political vision is one that people will identify with and support at the ballot box, you have to understand what wellbeing looks like for them. Which leads to an important question: do we actually even know what makes people happy?

Whatever makes you happy

In 1972, the Dragon King Jigme Singye Wangchuck of the tiny Himalayan nation of Bhutan gave a speech in which he coined the term 'gross national happiness', declaring it to be more important than gross national product (the more usual measure of economic prosperity).[3] In most places this would probably have been written off as a nice piece of political rhetoric. In Bhutan, where the transition from absolute monarchy to even basic democracy was still 25 years away, the King's words were taken very seriously and the royal sociologists set about trying to define what this might mean in practice. Parallels with work in the psychology departments of western universities quickly became apparent, and the modern study of wellbeing was born.

Over the next 40 years, a significant body of research has built up around the subject of how people rate their own happiness, what factors influence it, and how it varies between nations, social groups, places, and circumstances. Two main approaches have emerged. The 'subjective wellbeing' measure is the simplest, and involves asking people about their life and how they feel about it. Questions can look at both day-to-day emotional state ('how happy do you feel at the moment?') and longer term life satisfaction ('how happy are you with your life as a whole?'). The other approach involves looking at those factors which are believed to influence wellbeing (education, health, income, relationships, environment, etc.) and adding them up to give an overall score. Both methods have their strengths and weaknesses. The first approach is obviously subjective but it does have the advantage of measuring wellbeing directly. The second is more objective and can be calculated from available statistics, but it depends on understanding the links between wellbeing and circumstances, which are themselves hotly debated.

The work has polarised opinion about its value, how to apply it, and whether it should even be done at all. As far back as 1968, Senator Robert F. Kennedy gave a speech in which he said that 'gross national product ... measures everything, in short, except that which makes life worthwhile'.[4] In 2010, when the British government announced a decision to start collecting wellbeing statistics on a national basis, one Euro-MP called it 'voodoo sociology in the service of a bigger and more interfering state'.[5] In 2011, the United Nations urged countries 'to pursue the elaboration of additional measures that better capture the importance of the pursuit of happiness and well-being in development with a view to guiding their public policies'.[6] And in 2015 Gus (now Lord) O'Donnell, former head of the Civil Service, recommended that future governments should choose their policies by weighing the costs against the wellbeing benefits that they are expected to bring.[7]

Is it really possible to make sense of why people give the answers that they do and what factors contribute to their sense of wellbeing (or otherwise)? The answer is increasingly 'yes'. We do now have a good understanding of the factors which contribute towards wellbeing and, for the sake of my neighbours, the sooner we start to take notice of them the better.

The landscape of life

Wherever you go in the world and whoever you talk to, some things never change. Statistics must of course be recognised for what they are: everyone is an individual, and none of these conclusions can be used to stereotype how any particular person will think or feel. All of us will know exceptions to these 'rules', and may even be tempted to believe that the exception means that the rule is wrong. But the plural of anecdote is not data. When you ask the same questions of large groups of people rather than just a few individuals, similar patterns always begin to emerge.

People in good health feel better about life than those suffering from chronic illnesses (no surprises there). Women generally feel slightly happier about the overall state of their lives than men do, but are also more likely to be feeling anxious at any particular moment in time.

The relationship between age and happiness follows a well established pattern sometimes referred to as the 'U-bend' (because it follows the shape of a letter 'U' when plotted on a graph). Young people and the elderly are generally the happiest, with the lowest scores for wellbeing being recorded in middle age. It seems that younger people on average are optimistic about the future and have the time and freedom to pursue personal enjoyment day-to-day. Older people gradually become more content with their circumstances (or at least resigned to them), and may face fewer remaining uncertainties in life. Those in middle age by comparison are often at the peak of pressures imposed by developing a career, raising a family, and financial commitments. Although the U-bend is thankfully not too deep, the lowest point for pressure in the moment and concern about the future occurs for most people during their forties. Yes, the mid-life crisis is a real phenomenon and it shows up clearly in the wellbeing statistics.

This is all interesting stuff, but as a politician there is not much that I can do about people's age or gender. Of much more interest are the factors which are open to influence and which have a proven effect on wellbeing. These fall into three basic categories: security, prosperity, and relationships.

Warm and safe

The first big influence on wellbeing is physical safety and security. It is hard to feel good about life if your nation is being invaded or terrorised, your community is in the grip of gun and knife crime, or your government is a rapacious dictatorship with no regard for any rights but its own. Unsurprisingly the statistics are a bit harder to come by in this area. Governments and other agencies normally have more important things to do in the middle of a refugee crisis or a drug war than conduct wellbeing surveys (and the dictators don't seem that keen either). But we would be foolish to ignore the importance of safety and security as a basic foundation for human flourishing.

The most primitive form of government is a security pact. Strong rulers appear initially to protect their people against aggression (or sometimes to perpetrate it). We see this type of society right throughout history. Even in our so-called 'modern' world, that willingness to give up almost any other rights and privileges in return for basic security is never far beneath the surface. As soon as you take away the influence of a functioning state, it will be replaced almost immediately by strong-man generals, Afghan chieftains, Somali warlords, or urban gangsters.

Even in stable societies, fear of crime leads to anxiety which directly damages people's sense of wellbeing. Oddly enough, people's fear of crime is only loosely connected to the actual likelihood of them experiencing it. It is a feature of modern Britain that fear of crime has gone up even as the probability of becoming a victim of crime has fallen. It is clear that where people believe they are not safe walking the streets their wellbeing takes a knock – and they are quick to demand that 'someone' should do 'something' about it.

It's the economy, stupid

The second big influence on wellbeing is material prosperity. It should be obvious that living in poverty makes life miserable. The whole of our modern economic system is based on exactly this understanding: that money and the goods and services it can buy will make society a better and happier place for people to live their lives. Economic growth is thus seen as the key test of any government once basic physical security has been provided for. The idea of recession (where economic output goes down instead of up) has become synonymous with fear and failure – and a rapid change of government if not swiftly corrected.

Real material poverty seriously damages your wellbeing. People who have to walk miles to access dirty, polluted water supplies rarely say that they enjoy the exercise. Those living with an empty belly due to lack of food can think of little else. Watching your children suffer or die through easily preventable diseases or inadequate shelter to protect them from the elements is the most agonising experience a parent can undergo. To those of us fortunate enough to live in the rich world, this kind of absolute poverty sounds like something from the history books. But for millions of people around the globe, it is a horrific daily reality.

In spite of the many challenges still to be faced, it is impossible to deny the huge advances that have been made in tackling material poverty through simple economic growth. It took Europe and North America several centuries to eliminate the worst excesses of material poverty. In China, India, South-East Asia, and South America, around 2 billion people have been lifted out of absolute poverty through economic growth achieved by free markets, capital investment, and rising labour productivity in the last few decades alone.

Given the huge benefits it has brought to society through the elimination of poverty, most of us intuitively believe that when it comes to material wealth, more is better. We may say that 'money can't buy happiness', but the whole of our economic system is based on the assumption that it can and it does. If this is true, then we would expect to see a direct relationship between wealth and wellbeing. Surely the richer you are, on average the better you will feel about your life.

But this is where the story takes a sudden twist. If the relationship between age and wellbeing resembles a U-bend, the graph of wellbeing against material wealth looks more like a wheel ramp. As you would expect, at the beginning it rises swiftly. As the extreme effects of material poverty are removed from people's lives, their wellbeing rapidly increases. But at some point around low to average wealth and income, people discover that they now have all the basic necessities of life available to them: food, water, sanitation, shelter, basic healthcare and education, adequate income, and security for the young, elderly, and vulnerable. Somewhere around this point of material sufficiency there is a sharp kink in the curve and it goes almost flat. And if this wasn't enough, in rich economies there is almost no connection at all between further economic growth and improvements in average life satisfaction.

What this means is that there really is such a thing as 'enough'. Different individuals continue to experience different levels of wellbeing, but once they have reached what we might call the 'point of enough' there is no longer any real connection between wellbeing and wealth. The seriously rich can be extremely content in their comfortable lifestyle, or they can be stressed and depressed by the pressures of wealth and of maintaining it. Likewise, people living just above the point of enough may spend their days anxiously striving for more, or blissfully enjoying a lifestyle of relaxed simplicity.

This result is so surprising, and so counter to the assumptions that underpin our materialistic consumer society, that many people simply ignore it. If it came from just one or two studies you might be inclined to agree with them. But in fact it shows up in almost every study, in every place, however you ask the question and however you analyse the answers. An extra pound of wealth simply does not buy an extra point of wellbeing. It is, however, fair to say that increasing wealth is unlikely to make you miserable; some studies do show a weak increase and others are pretty much flat, but few seen to claim a negative correlation.

The implications of this are enormous. To understand what a big deal this really is, you only have to consider the basic principles of economics. Economist John Sloman starts his standard university textbook with the following statement: 'The central economic problem is the problem of scarcity … Ask people if they would like more money and the vast majority would answer "yes". They want more money so that they can buy more goods and services; and this applies not only to poor people but also to most wealthy people too. Even people living in a large well-furnished house and with an expensive car would probably like a bigger house, a second or third car, a villa on the Mediterranean, a luxury yacht, and so on. The point is that human wants are virtually unlimited.'[8]

While Sloman may be right about human wants, there is abundant evidence that these wants are basically misguided. People may say that they want more of this or that, but go back to the same group of people a year later and ask them whether they are any happier as a result and the answer will invariably be 'no'. This is not just theory or wishful thinking; it is an observable fact, which is now as robustly demonstrated as many of the other facts on which modern economics depends.

The fact that the connection between wealth and wellbeing stops at the point of enough is massively good news. If greater wealth automatically led to greater wellbeing, then the future of humanity would eventually come down to an endless fight over limited resources. But if wellbeing can be achieved by tackling poverty and getting everyone past the point of enough, then there is a real prospect that our planet could yet prove to have sufficient for all.

While material prosperity was bound to figure in any understanding of wellbeing, no-one, from Senator Kennedy to the Dragon King of Bhutan, has ever believed it to be the whole story. And our investigation of the connection between wellbeing and wealth does leave us with some important questions unanswered. Why do at least some studies of wellbeing show a further increase with greater wealth, even after the point of enough? Why do people in the same place and with the same income report such different levels of wellbeing? And why does the actual level of the point of enough seem to vary from place to place when basic human needs are pretty much the same the whole world over?

Friends and relations

The third and final driver of wellbeing is the quality of our relationships. It is said that no-one ever had written on their tombstone 'I wished I had spent more time at the office'. When people talk about what matters to them most, their answers almost always focus on people rather than possessions.

The vital importance of relationships comes through loud and clear in the studies that have been carried out. Starting with the closest relationships, people who are married are on average more satisfied with their lives than those who are not.[9] Commitment matters; living with a partner makes you happier than being single but not to the same extent as marriage. Those who are currently separated or divorced are on average unhappier still. People who have children are more satisfied with their lives overall but not necessarily less anxious; it seems that the sense of fulfilment that comes from raising a family is real and genuine, but so are the day-to-day pressures of parenthood.

Moving beyond the immediate family, exactly the same effect can be seen in relationships with a wider community. The number of personal friends you associate with is a more accurate indicator of wellbeing than the size of your personal income.[10] One 2006 survey[11] compared participation in community activities between a 'low life satisfaction' group of nations and a 'high life satisfaction' group, with other factors such as income, life expectancy, and development status being equal. Active participation in community activities was on average twice as high in countries with high life satisfaction compared to those with lower scores. A similar pattern shows up whatever type of activity people get involved in. Particularly noticeable are participation in churches (23% in high life satisfaction nations against 7% in the low life satisfaction group); sports and cultural activities (13% against 6%); groups supporting the young and elderly (8% against 3%); and political parties (7% against 4%). The only exception is trade union involvement, which was actually lower in high life satisfaction nations (6% against 10%). Presumably the role taken by unions in fighting against poor working conditions means that they are more active in places where working life is difficult to start with.

Relationships are so important that they continue to influence wellbeing even when they are indirect. Victorian Prime Minister Benjamin Disraeli looked at the condition of poor industrial workers in Britain and concluded that the rich and poor had become 'Two nations … who are as ignorant of each other's habits, thoughts, and feelings, as if they were dwellers in different zones, or inhabitants of different planets'.[12] He regarded this breach of relationship as not just a moral scandal, but a threat to the unity of the nation and ultimately its survival.

Disraeli's observations have survived in the concept of 'relative poverty'. As mentioned previously, defining poverty in developed nations is trickier than it first appears. At the end of our street there is an estate of houses and flats built cheaply and quickly by the local council in the 1970s. A fair number of the occupants live on low incomes or state benefits, which means that some of my neighbours would definitely be considered 'poor' by British standards. Yet, unlike many people throughout the world they clearly have access to all of the basic necessities of life. The UK Government currently defines 'relative poverty' as living on less than 60% of average income.[13] This can produce some rather perverse statistics. Following the 2008 financial crash average incomes dipped sharply, and because of this the number of people earning less than 60% of average actually went down. Any measure which says that poverty is reducing because people are earning less is bound to be treated with a degree of scepticism. Relative poverty doesn't actually measure poverty at all, it measures inequality, but it still matters because somewhere around that 60% level people start to feel that they have sufficiently less than their neighbours that the 'two nation divide' begins to re-emerge.

This idea that inequality drives a wedge through relationships explains why the point of enough can seem to fall at different places in different societies. If everyone around me lives in a simple home with access to a village school and clinic and grows food for sale at the local market, I will feel adequately prosperous if I have the same. If all my neighbours have cars, foreign holidays, and the trappings of a consumer lifestyle I will appear poor if I lack them; not because I am experiencing the actual negative effects of material poverty, but because I am excluded from the activities, experiences, and conversations that the rest of society engages in. My physical needs are met but my relationships are impoverished. The same principle probably explains why some surveys do show a continuing connection between individual wealth and wellbeing.[14] People are not made any happier by the material things that wealth can buy, but they may experience less social alienation and higher 'relational status' as they move further out of the zone of relative poverty.

The two-nation divide is not just caused by riches and poverty. Wherever society is divided between black and white, male and female, or high and low status, two nations can emerge. After the referendum vote, commentators are already identifying a new fault line in British society that separates the mostly young, urban, well qualified, and globally open from the older, more nativist, and globally closed. We are right to be concerned about these cultural divides in our society, but the picture becomes even more stark when they become entrenched by corrupt governments or legal systems. Countries which rank highly on respected international indexes for freedom, good governance, and equality under law consistently report higher wellbeing scores than those which do not. This is true even in nations with high average incomes where social division and exclusion does not necessarily lead to material poverty; the damage it does to relationships is enough.[15]

Where now after Brexit?

The purpose of governments is the wellbeing of their people. Where democratic governments fail to deliver happiness and wellbeing, there is a real risk that society will slide down the ever steepening slope of cynicism, disengagement, populism, dictatorship, and oppression. The Brexit vote was just the beginning of this process. It provided about the clearest possible expression of public disaffection and anger with things as they were, but none of these problems can be solved simply by leaving the EU. The key question now is 'where next for the UK'? If we can find a way to restore the sense of wellbeing which has been lost then the decision to leave the EU could prove to be a once-in-a-generation opportunity for positive, radical change. If not then the next offer is likely to be something even more extreme than the anti-immigrant, anti-establishment rhetoric which characterised much of the 'Leave' campaign.

The components of wellbeing are surprisingly simple and increasingly well understood. People feel satisfied with their lives when they are safe and secure, have sufficient material wealth to escape the effects of poverty, and live in an environment where personal and community relationships can flourish.

What sounds simple in theory has proved incredibly elusive in practice. Governments have at various times managed to deliver some of these things but they have never achieved all of them. The promotion of wellbeing should be a key priority of any government, but it cannot be an exclusive responsibility and it is clearly far too big a task to tackle alone. Governments thus need two things to progress in their mission: humility to recognise that they cannot succeed on their own, and allies to help them on the journey. And it is to this search for allies that we must turn next.

2

RELEASE THE
THREE ACTORS

Government is not reason; it is not eloquent; it is force. Like fire, it is a dangerous servant and a fearful master.

GEORGE WASHINGTON

I had to abandon free market principles in order to save the free market system.

GEORGE W. BUSH

It was February 1991, and Britain was shin-deep in 'The Wrong Kind Of Snow'. The rail system was already at a standstill, and a hapless spokesman for British Rail was about to offer the infamous excuse which would make him and his organisation a laughing stock for the next 20 years.

From the complete absence of cars on the main road outside, it appeared that the whole of Thurrock had already decided to take the day off. Tempting though it was to stay in bed, I didn't really feel that I had that option. At the time I was an engineer working at West Thurrock power station, and it was obvious that unless some of us managed to get to work people would soon be facing the arctic conditions without power or heating.

After trudging through snowdrifts for over an hour, I was amazed to discover that about half of the staff had somehow made it in to work. Virtually everyone within walking distance had trekked in, and most of the night shift had remained at their posts too. We now stood a fighting chance of keeping the plant running, but there was still the weather to contend with. I headed up to the feeder floor where I was stunned to discover two electricians with shovels busily digging snow off a frozen coal feeder.

To understand quite what a miracle this was, you have to have worked in nationalised industry. Electricians would never pick up a shovel. Shovelling was an Auxiliary Plant Attendant's job, and the Transport and General Workers Union would have been onto the Electrician's union like a shot if anyone had crossed the sacred line of job demarcation. But today, it seemed that all bets were off.

West Thurrock power station in 1991 was operated by the Central Electricity Generating Board; a state monopoly which generated virtually all of Britain's electrical power. My experience on that snowy day encapsulated much of what is best and worst about the state sector. The fact that so many staff had battled through the snow to get into work exemplifies the spirit of public service which genuinely drove us. At the same time, that spirit was in sharp contrast to how the industry usually ran. On a more normal day, things were constantly held up by self-imposed bureaucracy and a myriad of self-serving rules and wheezes. Later that same year the industry was privatised, and within two years the total staff of the successor company had come down by 50%. New technology played a part, but much of the change came from getting rid of complex and restrictive working practices which had built up over the years, conveniently buried in the nation's electricity bills.

Trust Busters

The 2016 EU referendum showed that trust in both the free market and the state was now comprehensively shattered. People undoubtedly voted against a European Union which they saw as distant, out of touch, bureaucratic, self-serving, and unrepresentative of their wants and needs. But they also voted against a political class which they increasingly held in utter contempt, believing it to be institutionally corrupt, following the parliamentary expenses scandal of 2009, and deaf to their concerns over issues like immigration, inequality, and rapid social and economic change. They voted against a capitalist world order which had proved itself catastrophically flawed during the 2008 financial crisis, and was seen as increasingly concentrating power and wealth in the hands of an unaccountable elite who were sucking communities and nations dry while not even having the decency to pay their taxes. They voted against a media whom they no longer trusted to act with integrity or tell the truth, public figures whose carefully managed personas might conceal a dark history of abuse, a police force who would conspire to cover up their own misdeeds, and a legal system that they felt ignored the cries of victims while bending over backwards to grant criminals their human rights.

The vote to leave the EU wasn't just a vote against European institutions, it was a vote of no confidence in almost every institution that underpins British society. Even democracy itself was regarded with suspicion: conspiracy theories that the referendum would be either rigged or re-run if it didn't deliver the 'right' answer abounded, and in the days running up to the poll there was a serious social media campaign encouraging voters to take a pen with them to the polling station, as the fact that British voters are traditionally provided with a pencil to mark their ballot paper obviously 'proved' that someone planned to rub out your preference and change it to the one that the authorities wanted.

This crisis of confidence comes at the worst possible time, because the very institutions which we will be depending on to help us chart a new course for post-Brexit Britain are the same ones that people voted against and no longer trust to do their job. And although the crisis is undoubtedly severe, it does give us an opportunity to re-think which 'actors' we should trust with each aspect of the changes that are needed to deliver our national wellbeing, and how we can move on from the outdated ideas of left vs right, state vs market, and socialism vs capitalism, which still dominate our political thinking.

Actor #1: The State

In the pursuit of national wellbeing, the state clearly has a role to play. In a democracy, that role can quickly start to feel all encompassing. If someone has a problem, the government should fix it. If something bad happens, the government should pass a law against it. If someone is in need of anything, the government should provide it. If something is too expensive, the government should make it cheaper. If things aren't the way they used to be, the government should turn back the clock. And so on. Politicians are pretty much complicit in this endless game of impossible expectations. Few government ministers have the courage to go on TV and say something to the effect of 'you know what, I'm not going to do anything. Sure it's a problem, but it's not one the government can solve. If I pretend that I have the answers then I will be giving you false hope and will probably make matters worse'. Instead we promise an endless stream of public inquiries, new laws, increased regulations, and additional services, all aimed at deflecting the criticism that we did nothing (and therefore obviously don't care).

To understand the role of the state properly we have to work out what it is uniquely capable of doing, then trust it to get on and do it. Going back to our drivers of wellbeing, the state is the only institution that can really enforce security and stability, using force if necessary. Citizens' militias have a long record of involvement in popular rebellions and insurgencies, and if all goes well they may even earn the title 'freedom fighters'. But no-one has ever found them anything other than a liability in winning the peace. The lesson of history is that private armies and vigilantes can tear down but they cannot build up. The de-nationalisation of public industries and services has been a hot political topic in the UK for three decades, but no-one has ever seriously suggested privatising the army or the police force.

The second area where the state is uniquely competent is in making rules and enforcing them. We pretty much take it for granted that a nation needs one set of laws and rules, and that someone will take responsibility for making sure that everyone follows them. What we forget is how easily this deal can break down if any part of the system fails. If the laws are not there or are not fit for purpose, everyone does their own thing. If they are not enforced (or if the enforcers are corrupt or negligent in their task) then bribery and lawlessness become rampant. If people do not basically support them then even the best enforcement will struggle to cope ('if no-one else is going to play by the rules then why should I?').

One of the most surprising charity initiatives I have come across is 'project Umubano'. Alongside other more obvious humanitarian work, Umubano took the unusual step of sending teams of legal professionals to Sierra Leone, an African country torn by ten years of civil war. You might think that the last thing a poor, traumatised nation would want or need was a bunch of lawyers. Yet the Umubano volunteers did invaluable work in helping local people to rebuild, not just with bricks and mortar, but the basic structures of civil institutions and the legal system. Both wellbeing and economic development are proven to be directly connected to strong government institutions and the rule of law.

The third area where the state has a unique role to play is in collective responsibility. To understand this role, you only have to walk a short distance from our house to an estate of 1930s bungalows nearby. The area is full of character, with many of the homes beautifully renovated and surrounded by spacious gardens. However, the roads are shocking; by far the worst in town. Because the estate is privately owned, the upkeep of the roads is the responsibility of the householders themselves. Every so often someone will suggest that everyone contributes towards repairs, but inevitably a few people refuse. Others then withdraw because they consider it unfair that they should pay up while their neighbours contribute nothing. Finally the scheme collapses, and increasingly, so do the roads. In the rest of town by contrast, the roads are maintained to a fairly decent standard. These roads are 'adopted' by the local council, repairs are paid for by everyone through taxation, and the worst bits are done on an annual programme based on their condition.

Roads are just one example of facilities that everyone uses (or might use) but no-one owns. Paying for food, clothing, or mobile phones is straightforward for most people; if I want it and can afford it, I buy it. Paying for the police, the army or the national fisheries protection service is more difficult. I may want the benefits they provide (or at least I may want to avoid what would happen if they were absent), but I don't use them directly and I am unlikely to make a voluntary contribution unless others do the same. The answer is that everyone pays something through taxation. Where benefits are collective then responsibility has to be collective too. With its unique authority to make the rules, and hence the power to force people to pay their taxes, the state is an essential enabler for services of this type.

Actor #2: The Market

There is a story (and I would love to believe it is true) that in the early 1980s, a delegation of officials from Soviet Russia came to visit the Greater London Council. After a day viewing the capital's landmarks, one of the Russians asked if he could meet the man who was responsible for the great city's food supplies. Imagine his surprise when he was told that no such person existed.

Russia at the time had the most comprehensive system of centralised planning ever devised. Collective farms grew crops in accordance with instructions issued to them five years in advance, and food was allocated, processed and distributed through a vast network of official organisations. While most of the people managed to get fed most of the time, the end result was often characterised by long queues, poor quality, and limited choice. In London by contrast, there was no day-to-day central planning at all. People relied entirely on market forces to ensure that everything from staples to luxuries would somehow be there on the shelves when they decided to buy them. Food queues were not a feature of London life then or now, and the city enjoyed one of the most varied, cosmopolitan and international diets in the world.

The first great strength of markets is that they manage enormous complexity, brilliantly. Every day, London wakes up and decides that it wants organic muesli; sausage, bacon and eggs; kosher bagels; coffee and croissants; or champagne and wild strawberries for breakfast. And every day, somehow, all of these wants are delivered onto the plates of hungry Londoners. London gets through over 30 million meals and snacks a day, made up from well over 100 million food items. These are provided by supply chains which touch every part of the world. A banana grower in the West Indies sells her produce to a buyer from an American fruit company. A truck takes the bananas to a transit shed where they are loaded into a refrigerated container. A bulk container ship built in South Korea carries them to the port of Tilbury in Thurrock, where a crane driver loads them onto a train to be moved to a warehouse in the British Midlands. Here the container is opened and bananas go to a distribution centre belonging to one of the big supermarket chains. A computer system in a global data centre in India tells the warehouse that a convenience supermarket in Thurrock is running low on bananas, and fresh supplies are automatically loaded onto the overnight delivery run. As the crane driver in Tilbury comes off shift, his brother the London cabbie buys a banana for his packed lunch, before driving the 20 miles down the A13 to start his day ferrying international agricultural commodity traders around London's financial district. One down, ninety-nine million nine hundred and ninety-nine thousand nine hundred and ninety-nine to go. And yet it works, every day, with a phenomenally high success rate.

The second power of markets is perhaps even more surprising. They reveal the truth. This is by no means immediately obvious, given the lengths that some people will go to in order to strike a deal. Three thousand years ago, King Solomon wrote that "'It's no good, it's no good!" says the buyer; then off he goes and boasts about his purchase.'[16] The basic working of markets has changed little since Solomon's day. When you listen to two people haggling over a price you might find it hard to believe that they are talking about the same item, let alone that they are engaged in a shared quest for truth. But in fact, regardless of the posturing and arguing, at the point that a deal is finally struck we know one thing with absolute certainty. At that moment, the buyer was willing to pay that price and the seller was willing to accept it. Hands are shaken and a deal is done. And off goes the buyer and boasts about her purchase on social media (until she gets home and starts to have second thoughts).

Imagine that I arrive at Fenchurch Street station (as made famous by the London Monopoly board) late one evening, to discover that the last train to Essex has been cancelled. Outside the station our London cabbie, his lunchtime banana long since eaten, is sitting at the cab rank waiting for the final fare of the day. I stick my head through his window and ask him:

'How much for a ride back to Stanford-le-Hope in Essex?'
'At this time of night, mate, all the way out there? You're talking sixty quid at least.'
'Sixty? That's ridiculous. The train only costs me thirteen quid return.'
'Yeah, but the train's not running, is it?'
'OK, but I can get the District Line to Upminster and call my wife to pick me up from there. That's going to cost me a lot less than sixty.'
'Well look, I've got to head home that way anyway, I'll do you a deal. Forty-five.'
'If you're driving out to Essex anyway then this is a bonus from your point of view. Twenty-five maximum.'

And so it goes on. Eventually I hand over £30 cash and the taxi heads out through the East End and home to Essex. What was the truth in this situation? Maybe my daughter was sick in bed and my wife would not have been willing to leave her, in which case I would have had little choice but to pay the £60 if the cabbie had stuck out for it. Maybe he lives just round the corner from me, in which case even £10 would have been extra money in his pocket for no extra effort and he might have been happy to take it. We will never know, but what we do know is this: on that evening, £30 was acceptable to both parties. That statement at least, is absolutely true.

The cabbie may moan to me on the way home about the rising price of bananas, but he still chose to pay it this morning rather than buying apples instead. His words say that the price is unacceptable but his actions reveal the truth. My evening newspaper may tell me that the port of Tilbury and the dock workers' union are in dispute about crane drivers' wages, but the truth is that the cabbie's brother won't quit his job even if he doesn't get a pay rise this year. This ability constantly to find and test the truth about what people will and won't do is what enables markets to feed the city of London, distribute the right number of bananas to every point on the planet, and get me and a hundred other people safely home when our train is cancelled, despite the mind-boggling complexity that each of these challenges involves.

The third ability of markets is to release creativity and innovation. It has been said that 'if you build a better mousetrap, the world will beat a path to your door'.[17] We like to think that all of the great strides in improving human society have been made for altruistic reasons, but in fact many have come about because someone saw an opportunity to develop a successful product. That's not in any way to criticise the motives of those pioneers; they may well have chosen to enter that particular field because they saw the wider social benefits it could bring. But ultimately the success of their endeavours was determined by the response of the market to their invention.

I have read a lot of books as I prepared to write this one, often on the train from Stanford-le-Hope to London Fenchurch Street. If you were to ask my fellow commuters what they would choose to do with their 50 minutes of enforced idleness twice a day, they might say something like browse a newspaper, read a classic novel, or prepare mentally for the day ahead. However, the truth (remember the power of markets to reveal truth?) turns out to be that they actually prefer to look at embarrassing pictures of what their mates did last night. This in turn has led to an astonishing growth in smartphone handsets, software applications to run on them, and networks of masts and fibre-optic cables to connect them. It has also made the developers of Facebook (a social networking site) extremely wealthy. And while it is debatable whether easy access to pictures of drunken friends or amusing cats has made any obvious contribution to improving the human condition, the same mobile application technology is quietly revolutionising everything from banking to medicine to traffic management.

Steamships replaced sail because they could move goods and people around the world's oceans faster and more cheaply. They say that the American West was won from the saddle of a horse, but it was the invention of refrigeration and air conditioning that enabled dusty frontier towns to develop into modern cities. Put the two together and you were at last able to transport perishable items over international distances – and the modern banana trade was born.

Actor #3: The Community

The state regards people as 'citizens'; defined in terms of a set of rights and duties. The market sees them as producers and consumers; components in an economic system acting out of rational self-interest. Community understands people through their relationships with others.

In 1999 the port of Tilbury saw a surge of ethnic Albanian refugees, arriving in the back of lorries after a harrowing journey across half of Europe. Most were fleeing from fighting in the former Yugoslav province of Kosovo, and the refugees included young teenage boys travelling alone, sent by parents desperate to avoid them getting caught up in the atrocities being committed against anyone suspected of being a rebel fighter.

Reception in the local community was mixed. Some were resentful of the additional burden on social housing and welfare services caused by the newcomers. Others wanted to do something to help, and a local church started to open its doors as a kind of impromptu community centre. The churchgoers offered food, hospitality, clothing and other essentials, and basic English lessons.

Friendships quickly developed, and these were reinforced through the international language of football when the 2001 World Cup qualifying games between the two nations were projected on big screens to a packed Anglo-Albanian audience.

When some of the refugees decided to return and rebuild their villages, an entire articulated lorry full of aid was donated and driven out by volunteers from Thurrock to help them. In 2004, my wife and I had the privilege of travelling with our two young children to help run a youth camp in the mountains of western Kosovo. Conditions were extremely basic, the country remained under NATO military control, and we were a long way from help if anything had gone wrong. But just as our community had opened its arms in welcome five years previously, we were now received in that same spirit. It was humbling to spend time with children and young people who had lived through the horrors of war and its aftermath, and were now learning to enjoy life and peace once more.

The market is powerless to explain the connections that formed between Thurrock and Kosovo in the early 2000s. Little money changed hands and no-one made a profit out of what took place. Similarly, the state saw the situation as a 'refugee crisis' and nothing more. The government fulfilled its obligations under international treaties and provided support, without which people would have struggled to survive. But the community shared in and understood the trauma of war, the desperation of exile, the hope of return, and the challenges of rebuilding a new life.

Secondly, community provides the foundation on which other institutions sit. Kosovo descended into war in 1998 because the Serbian authorities had ceased to enjoy the confidence of the majority Albanian population. The state could continue to project power through its soldiers and militias, but it could no longer truly govern a population which refused to recognise its legitimacy. Without the consent of the community, government is reduced to control and subjugation. Equally damaging was the collapse of the economy during the war and its aftermath. Markets are a universally understood principle, but without the foundations of a functioning community they quickly retreat to the most basic bartering of essentials. No-one is going to invest in property which may be seized or destroyed tomorrow. You cannot form a stable business relationship with a neighbour with whom you may find yourself at war this time next week.

Finally, community provides an environment in which non-financial costs and benefits can be valued and non-statutory rights and responsibilities can be exercised. Most of the trickiest problems in economics are caused by transactions where some of the consequences have a financial value but some do not. Economists call these 'externalities', and we will be encountering them again later. Robert F. Kennedy put it this way: 'gross national product does not allow for the health of our children, the quality of their education, or the joy of their play. It does not include the beauty of our poetry or the strength of our marriages; the intelligence of our public debate or the integrity of our public officials. It measures neither our wit nor our courage; neither our wisdom nor our learning; neither our compassion nor our devotion to our country.'[18] Only the community possesses the human and relational resources to manage the tension between these issues in a holistic way.

A few miles from where I live, Europe's largest and most modern container port and logistics park is rising from the mud of the Thames estuary at London Gateway. When fully operational it will handle millions of containers per year and employ over twelve thousand people. The market has had a huge influence on where and how the port is built. Market forces dictated that a new port must go on a deep estuary to handle the largest and most efficient container ships. It should be located close to London, western Europe's biggest consumer market. The market determines how many people are employed, what they get paid, what cargoes come though the port, where they end up, how much is charged for them, and how they travel on to their destination.

The state has played a big role too. A lengthy public enquiry was held before permission to build was granted, and dozens of conditions were applied. An entire area of land further up the river has been given back to the sea to replace the tidal mud flats which were being lost, and is now managed as a nature reserve. Thousands of snakes, lizards and amphibians were relocated to new habitats before construction could commence. Roads have been built and widened, landscaping planted, and acoustic barriers erected to try to reduce the impact of heavy lorries on nearby houses.

But even after every market force has been responded to and every legal condition complied with, you would not have a complete picture of the impact that London Gateway Port is having on our town. After years of declining traffic into the oil refineries, Corringham is about to become a lot busier. Will the older, retired generation decide it is time to move away, and what effect will that have on extended families? Will the new jobs mean better prospects for our children, or will they look on as their town becomes a place that others drive past to get to work? If house prices rise, will that put more financial pressure on families and lead to further loss of green spaces and community facilities? Will the combined effect of all these things improve our sense of wellbeing, or will it consolidate Thurrock's position at the bottom of the list?

The market doesn't even attempt to place a value on all of these things. The state is concerned mostly with whether the rules are being followed. In our community, they are discussed in every pub, at every school gate, and at every door that we knock on at election time. From these thousands of conversations and from every real-life decision that is made as a result of them, our community will start to understand the deeper impacts of what is happening. Sometimes we will gladly accept the benefits that come our way. Other times we will come together and fight. And if our children are still living here 20 years from now, it will be these human issues and not the financial or legal ones that will largely shape their lives.

Rock, paper, scissors

Every schoolchild knows the game of rock, paper, scissors. The two players simultaneously choose from three simple symbols with their hands. Rock blunts scissors, scissors cut paper, paper wraps rock. It's a great way to settle arguments or make decisions, and sometimes I think that politicians should use it more often.

I'm not sure what symbols you could make for state, market, and community, but it is clear that they do influence each other both positively and negatively. At its simplest you might think that the state provides security, the market produces prosperity, and the community grows relationships. Each of the three actors has a role to play, and wellbeing is assured as a result. Reality is rather more complicated than that.

State creates market. The first markets grew up in places where the king's soldiers were present to prevent traders from being robbed by bandits and put anyone selling dodgy goods into the stocks for a bit of rough justice. Even modern, sophisticated markets depend ultimately on state regulation for their operation. The market in stocks and shares, which has been the main method for financing the growth of industrial economies, depends for its existence on the legal concept of the limited liability company. Limited liability allows investors to share in the profits without risking losses greater than what they put in. The stock market plays by its own powerful and complex rules, but it could not exist without the legal framework which shapes it and sets the parameters in which it operates.

Market constrains state. Every government comes to power promising some version of high growth, low inflation, full employment, a strong currency, low taxes, and generously funded public services. It could even pass a law which set a figure for all of those things. Unfortunately the market has a habit of ignoring laws like that. The state sets the environment in which markets operate, but it cannot determine the outcomes that they produce. In September 1992 Britain crashed out of the European Exchange Rate Mechanism, after the government had raised interest rates from 10% to 15% in a single day and spent £27 billion of foreign currency reserves to try and support the value of the pound. All their efforts failed. The market discerned the truth, and the truth was that the British currency was simply not sustainable at that level.

Community enables state and market. People cannot be governed in the long term without their consent, and they cannot be made to participate in markets indefinitely without their agreement. In the world today we can point to both brutal dictatorships which oppress their people and unfair trade systems which discriminate against poor producers. Some have lasted for decades, but they become a little more isolated each year. In the long term they will fall, just as communist dictatorships and the transatlantic slave trade fell before them.

Market and state displace community. The community is the most subtle of the actors in terms of the connections it forms and the range of factors it holds in balance, but it is also the most fragile. Where state and market advance, the community tends to retreat. For most of our history, children in Britain were raised and cared for by a community network of parents and grandparents, aunts and uncles, friends and neighbours. Rapid social change in the last 200 years disrupted these networks, and gaps began to emerge. The state responded by providing a safety net of welfare provision, and the market moved in to offer paid childcare services. With every advance, the network of community support was further weakened. Communities are reluctant to provide for themselves something which has come to be seen as a state responsibility or a traded commodity. All three actors are now heavily involved, but the total capacity has not increased as a result and many of the problems that the changes were supposed to solve still exist in different forms.

Putting them to work

During the twentieth century, the dominant view was that one actor would eventually prove stronger, fairer, and more competent than the others. All we needed to do was work out which one. Capitalists believed that the free market would deliver endless progress if the state just got out of the way and let them get on with it. Socialists, fascists, and communists may have disagreed violently with each other, but they all shared a basic belief that only a powerful state could provide the answers. The power of communities to solve their own problems when freed from the corrupting influences of wealth and power was championed by an equally unlikely mix of libertarians, communitarians, and environmentalists.

The EU referendum vote drew a line under all of these ideologies in their traditional forms. As a nation we no longer believe that capitalism will continue to deliver peace and prosperity if left to its own devices. We do not consider that our governments and international institutions are capable of solving all the challenges that we face. And we sense that our communities are under threat and already too weakened to solve their own problems.

Given their different strengths and abilities, it now seems very unlikely that any one actor is ever going to be up to the task of delivering wellbeing on their own. For every problem that we face and every opportunity that we see, we need to play each to their strengths while avoiding their weaknesses. The question is not 'which is best?', but 'which is best able?' to deliver this particular aspect of wellbeing.

We now know in general terms what it takes to encourage wellbeing and we know what actors are available to help deliver it. But specific problems demand specific solutions. We will now turn to the first of these; one which was a key driver of the unhappiness and disaffection which led directly to the referendum vote. What are the causes of unemployment and poverty, and what can we do about it?

3

ABOLISH UNEMPLOYMENT

A man can't do anything better than eat and drink and be satisfied
with his work.

THE BIBLE

Work is a necessary evil to be avoided.

MARK TWAIN

'Immigrants are coming to take your jobs!' This was the rallying
cry of the 'Leave' campaign, and the unspoken narrative
behind many of the points made during the referendum
debate. There is a housing shortage (because of immigration).
The health service is overstretched (because of immigration). It's
not safe to walk the streets at night (because of immigration). The
most controversial poster of the campaign showed a long queue
of migrants heading for the UK. It was powerfully evocative of
the famous 'Labour isn't working' poster from the 1979 general
election which showed a long snaking dole queue. The visual
message was clear: immigration for them equals unemployment
for you.

Most economists are sceptical of the idea that immigration
causes unemployment. They would argue that the truth is almost
the reverse of this: people come to the UK because their labour
and skills are needed, and they contribute more to the economy
in wealth creation, taxes, and money spent with local businesses
than they take out. Viewed nationally, every one who arrives
adds a fraction of a percent to economic growth and makes the

nation as a whole a little bit better off. But that's not the picture you hear when you knock on the doors of Thurrock at election time. Here it seems to be almost universally accepted that immigrants take away jobs and make ordinary people worse off. So who is right?

Not all doorstep discussions with voters are particularly edifying. There is a familiar conversation which every Thurrock politician knows all too well, that starts with 'I'm not a racialist but …' and then rapidly goes downhill into a rant about how foreigners are the cause of all our woes. However, I clearly remember one doorstep encounter with an unemployed plasterer in the run-up to the 2014 local elections. He still felt that immigration was putting the squeeze on jobs, but unlike many of his neighbours he could offer a clear explanation as to how and why. 'It's like this', he said. 'A few years ago I was working on sites in London and earning good money. Then the companies started bringing in Eastern Europeans who would work for about half of what British builders were getting. They can afford to do it because they come over for a few weeks or months at a time, share the cheapest accommodation they can find, and send the rest of the money home. There's no way I can live on that sort of money – I've got a family to feed and a mortgage to pay at UK prices. But what can I do? If I won't take a lower rate then the companies will just find another immigrant who will.'

It seems that the picture on the ground is more complicated than the economists with their net tax gains and national average effects are letting on. Migration creates winners and losers – and the losers are starting to hurt. If you have skills that are in demand then you have little to fear and much to gain from freedom of movement. But if you are deemed replaceable then it's a buyer's market, and that puts the squeeze on wages and ultimately on whether you can find a job at all.

We'll come back to the challenges of immigration later, but first there is an even bigger question to answer. Why do we have unemployment at all? After all, no-one ever put it in their election manifesto and no-one voted for it. To answer that question, we need to start in a place where poverty doesn't lurk in the complexities of minimum wages and marginal tax rates; it stares you right in the face.

The Chennai conundrum

One week into our stay in Chennai, Southern India, I took my life in my hands and agreed to have a go at driving the car. Chennai traffic has to be seen to be believed. Ox carts share the roads with Mercedes saloons, tiny three-wheeler auto-rickshaws dodge between massive Ashok Leyland trucks, and stately Hindustan Ambassadors (still based on a 1950s Morris Oxford) squeeze within inches of motorcycles carrying a family of four plus their shopping (but no helmets).

The streets are not the only bit of Chennai characterised by frantic activity. Pavements are crowded with stalls and shopfronts selling everything you can imagine: brightly coloured saris, jasmine garlands, fresh fruit and vegetables, packaged toiletries, pots and pans, and hot puri with dal. Larger stores are by comparison a haven of air-conditioned calm, staffed by a discrete army of uniformed security guards, greeters, assistants, clothing adjusters, gift wrappers, bag packers, and money takers. Away from the streets it seems that every spare corner from dingy basements to flat rooftops is filled with washers, cookers, makers, menders, dealers, and traders going about their business. And further still from prying eyes, the poorest and most desperate pick over stinking heaps of rubbish, hunting for a few kilos of metal or plastics they can sell to avoid going hungry tonight.

Our home for the next couple of weeks is a small maisonette in a normal Chennai suburb, occupied by a couple who run a local charity that we have come to visit. After a number of years spent building up a well-regarded orphanage, they are now responding to the devastation caused by the 2004 Indian ocean earthquake and tsunami. Our friends are not especially well off; by local standards they would be considered middle income at best. Yet in their modest home they employ a full-time cook and housemaid, a full-time driver, and a woman who comes in to do the washing and ironing.

Chennai clearly has huge poverty. Not the '60% of average income' kind, but the 'nowhere to sleep, nothing to eat, no money for medicine, can't afford to send the children to school' kind. What it doesn't really have is unemployment. All across the city every street, workshop, yard and slum is a hive of activity. Far too many are unskilled, poorly paid, or working in awful conditions, but everyone is doing something.

In Britain, by contrast, unemployment historically varies between 5% and 10%.[19] On a typical day over the last few decades, anywhere from 1.5 million to 3 million adults of working age have been sitting at home effectively doing nothing. To bring it closer to home, that means between 50 and 100 people on our small estate alone, and possibly quite a few more considering that the council flats tend to have above average levels of unemployment. Of course their condition is not nearly as desperate as their counterparts in Chennai. All of them have access to housing, healthcare, education, and a basic income provided by the state through the benefits system. Some will definitely be below the 60% relative poverty line, but all should have enough to ensure their wellbeing in purely material terms.

Unfortunately, material sufficiency isn't enough. In the 2012 UK happiness survey, whether you had a job or not was one of the single strongest indicators of wellbeing. People in unemployment were more than twice as likely to report low life satisfaction compared with those in work,[20] and the discrepancies cannot be explained away by differences in income alone. Long-term unemployment makes you miserable. It can also damage your marriage, harm your physical and mental health, affect your children's performance at school, erode your friendships, and spoil your sex life. Almost every component of wellbeing is affected, so it is hardly surprising that unemployment is a key focus of political debate.

Catch 22

Chennai has low unemployment but serious poverty. Thurrock has low material poverty by global standards but significant unemployment. Both seriously damage wellbeing. Is it ever possible to eliminate both?

Economics does not give us much cause for optimism. The employment market is a market just like any other. It follows the same basic laws of supply and demand. People with rare or difficult-to-acquire skills such as top lawyers and premiership footballers are in short supply and can command high wages as a result. In competitive environments it is even more pronounced. No-one wants to come second in a court case or a football match, and to win you have to hire the best. At the other end of the labour market, those with only basic qualifications have little to distinguish themselves from the next applicant. Employers have a wide choice of potential workers, which means they can offer low wages and still find someone to take the job.

This explains why wage levels in a free market can vary so massively, but it doesn't explain why unemployment exists. When I look round Thurrock, there is no shortage of jobs that need doing. Our local park has litter in it and the town centre could use some attention too. Long queues form at Stanford-le-Hope railway station when only one ticket counter is open, while two stops down the line at Tilbury you often see kids jumping over the fence to avoid buying a ticket at all because there is no security. Social care for the elderly is strictly rationed, offices no longer have the admin and support staff that they used to, and plumber's and fitter's mates are a thing of the past. Statistics show that those who do have a job are working longer hours, doing a wider range of tasks, and suffering more from stress than ever. So why in a society that is crying out for things to be done do we still have people sitting at home doing nothing?

Economists say that when everything being offered for sale in a particular market has found a buyer, the market has 'cleared'. For this to happen, the price has to be low enough to encourage just enough buyers to come in. The price where this occurs is called the 'market clearing price'.[21] If the wages being paid are low enough, the labour market will clear and there will be no unemployment. Our local park is scruffier than it could be because the council cannot afford to employ additional staff to maintain it. The queues at Stanford-le-Hope station are long for exactly the same reason. But what if we could employ park keepers for just £1 an hour? My children would have a safe and well maintained facility that they could enjoy, and both their health and relationships would benefit as a result. My office would employ an office junior to organise meetings and make the tea and coffee (rather than have highly paid contractors stopping work to do it themselves). My plumber would have a plumber's mate to fetch and carry stuff, lend a helping hand, and hopefully learn something on the job at the same time. Local businesses would take on apprentices and a whole generation would have access to the jobs and skills that they need to succeed in life.

Unemployment would be ended … but we would be back in the slums of Chennai. No-one can afford to live in Thurrock on wages of £1 an hour. That's £40 a week, and you couldn't even rent a single room for that, let alone manage to eat as well. You cannot pay wages low enough to clear the employment market without causing severe poverty of a kind that is unacceptable in any developed society (and ought to be unacceptable in any society). It seems that we are stuck in a trap. You can't have full employment without poverty, and you can't pay everyone a decent wage without causing unemployment.

It's better to have tried and failed …

With the market apparently powerless to end unemployment in an acceptable way, the other actors have stepped in to try and sort things out. Traditional communities rarely suffer from unemployment. Everyone in the village will join in to help water the fields, harvest the crops, raise barns, build houses, and whatever else needs to be done. Standards of living tend to be poor and life is often precarious, but at least everyone is poor together. In wellbeing terms, subsistence communities often fail to provide adequate material prosperity, but they do offer some security and a rich network of relationships, all regulated by the community itself.

The massive increase in material wellbeing that has come from economic development has always been accompanied by migration from the countryside to cities. The same pattern is seen in nineteenth-century Europe, twentieth-century South-East Asia, and twenty-first-century China. People move, not because they are forced to, but because they see the opportunity of a better life. Over a billion people have been lifted out of poverty in the last few decades alone by this type of economic growth. But it does come at a price. When the market advances, community retreats. The relational mechanisms which once found a means for everyone both to contribute and to benefit do not seem to survive the shock of rapid economic transition, and the poverty/unemployment trap is sprung.

State approaches to dealing with the problem take one of two forms. The state can either find work for people to do, or provide welfare payments to prevent them falling into complete poverty.

Government make-work schemes have a poor record. Infrastructure investment (such as building things like roads and power grids) makes sense while a nation is developing, but there is only a certain amount of infrastructure that the economy can productively use before a law of diminishing returns takes over. Propping up failing industries which would otherwise close tends to become a 'bottomless pit' and an unacceptable drain on public finances. Creating massive public sector bureaucracies and monopolies which offer stable employment breeds corruption and inefficiency; all of which has to be funded by taxing the more productive areas of the economy. At the time of writing, the nations which are still suffering most from the Euro zone sovereign debt crisis are those which took this route. They have accumulated huge levels of public debt to pay for their policies over a number of years, with no obvious method of ever paying it back. The problem is basically one of making good choices and managing complexity, as illustrated by the differences between Moscow's and London's food supply or the Central Electricity Generating Board's restrictive working practises. The Soviet system of centralised state control ensured that everyone had a job, but the end result was still poverty and oppression for millions.

With governments apparently unable to create sustainable work, the last resort has been to pay people to do nothing. This is the situation faced by nearly 2 million people in Britain today. The state sets a legal minimum wage which prevents the worst effects of working poverty for those in work. It also pretty much guarantees that the job market will never 'clear', and there will always be a significant level of unemployment.[22] As we have seen, this prevents destitution and for that it has to be seen as a good thing. But the long-term effects on wellbeing are catastrophic. Welfare payments keep poverty off the streets, but they are a very poor substitute for the wider benefits that come from being an active, productive member of society.[23] Not only that, but for many the situation can become self-perpetuating. Life without the structure, self-discipline, and social skills of work makes people progressively less able to cope with a job even if they can find one. Unskilled work pays little more than state benefits anyway, and it may cause you to lose other entitlements too. By the time you add in the costs of travel, work clothing, and so on, many people have actually found themselves worse off in low paid employment than if they had remained on welfare.

Financially we have found ourselves in a position where we spend billions of pounds a year paying people to do nothing, despite there being an abundance of things that need doing. It breeds resentment, harms wellbeing, and is incredibly wasteful. But what else can we do?

Let's get to work

We have seen that the work is there to be done, and we have seen that the money is there to pay people to do it (because the state continues to fund the welfare bill which is roughly equivalent to a basic wage). The problem is one of matching the people to the work and getting them to do it in a way which doesn't become a permanent drain on public funds. This is the kind of conundrum that markets ought to be really good at solving. It involves massive complexity, with millions of tasks to be performed and paid for every day. And it requires a heavy dose of truth telling: which jobs are we actually willing to pay to have done as a society, as opposed to those that people merely claim are most useful? But unfortunately, the labour market can't resolve it because while employers would be willing to pay something, that something is less than the minimum wage and less than the alternative of a life on benefits.

But what if the state and the market joined forces? I have already admitted that I would pay £1 an hour for a park keeper or an office junior, and when put under the truth-exposing light of the market it might even be £2 or £3. The state is already paying someone further along my street maybe £6 an hour in welfare benefits of various types. Put them together and we have a job that needs doing, someone to do it, and enough money to pay them. In fact when you add it all up we probably have a small surplus. This is to be expected, because while the unskilled worker may not be able to command a minimum wage in purely economic terms, their work would still add some value. At the moment they are contributing nothing. Get them into any form of productive employment and you will add billions of pounds of value to the economy; more than enough to ensure that everyone including employers, workers, and taxpayers can benefit as a result.

Here is how it might work in practice. The government changes the rules to say that if any company, small business, or self-employed person employs someone to work for them at a set minimum wage (say about £8 an hour),[24] they can claim the whole amount back off their tax bill.[25] This means that they effectively can get an employee for free. Of course they still have to pay the various overhead costs that come with employing someone, but these should come to no more than our hypothetical pound-an-hour. They get it as a tax deduction for two reasons; firstly because this makes the scheme almost free for the government to administer (companies are already filing tax returns and having their accounts audited anyway), and secondly because it's much harder to fiddle the system if it comes out of your own takings than if it arrives in the form of a cheque from the government.

This of course makes offering low wage jobs vastly more attractive to employers, and it runs the risk of creating a 'two tier' system with no opportunity for further reward or progression. To get round this, we can taper the tax deduction so that it falls off gradually as wages rise. Getting the 'slope' right will be a job for the economists (there may even be a Nobel Prize in it if someone can get it spot-on), but to illustrate the point, let's suggest that for every £1 extra the employer decides to pay, £2.00 of state subsidy will be withdrawn. So if the employee's wage is £1 higher at £9 per hour, the subsidy drops from £8.00 to £6.00. This means the employer is now paying £3.00 an hour in real terms. If salary rises to £10 per hour the employer will have to fund £6.00, and when it reaches £12.00 per hour the state subsidy will be gone altogether and the 'normal' free market takes over. Set the slope too steep and it will become unattractive to raise pay or have sensible pay differentials between jobs (and therefore to attract more capable staff to the more challenging roles). Set it too shallow and the taxpayer will be unable to afford the bill (although it may be possible to correct this by adjusting the wider tax system).[26]

The effect would be dramatic and immediate. Millions of new jobs would be created as companies took the opportunity of employing extra staff at minimal cost to themselves. International corporations that currently pay little tax on their UK operations will be incentivised to bring more of their profit back onshore, as without the tax liability to fund their wage subsidies they will struggle to compete with those able to benefit from lower salary costs. Businesses which already employ large numbers of low-paid workers would enjoy a short-term profits windfall; limited only by the fact that they cannot claim more in subsidy than they already pay in taxes. But the economists will tell us that this won't last long. They will rapidly experience more competition for staff (because there will be a lot more low-wage jobs out there) which means that wages paid to their employees will have to rise to keep hold of good people. The increased profitability will encourage new businesses to enter the market (expect rapid growth in the catering, light manufacturing, and service industries), and that will drive prices down. Profits will normalise again, but entire sections of the economy will have been enlarged and transformed as a result. And the curse of unemployment will be lifted from the shoulders of millions of people.

The devil in the detail

At a high level it is obvious that this scheme will work. The 'jobs' in the sense of useful work to be done already exist, and the 'wages' are already being paid by society in the form of unemployment benefits. By matching the two, we move millions of people out of economic inactivity and into at least partially productive employment, so the overall effect cannot be anything other than positive. Given the scale of the change it will be necessary to work hard at getting the detail right and allow time for markets to adapt by phasing the new system in over a transitional period, but the huge benefits to wellbeing that will result make it well worth the effort.

The first big challenge is to make sure that the public purse can afford it. To let the market do its job it is necessary to offer incentives to employ all low-paid workers, not just the 5–10% who might otherwise be unemployed. If the responsibility for paying everyone on minimum wages suddenly moved from employers to the state, the costs could be measured in billions even after factoring in the savings in benefits. However, this is where market forces start to work in our favour. There are millions of businesses who would like to benefit from virtually free employees (who wouldn't?), so the 'demand' will be high. Even with over a million of the formerly unemployed joining the labour market, the 'supply' remains limited. The inevitable market response is that the price goes up. In our example above, the lowest real-world wage would not be £8; it might stabilise at around £10. At this level the employer bears half of the cost themselves. This is still attractive to them, but it certainly isn't free labour.

The last resort is that any shortfall in the welfare savings and economic gains would have to be funded through business taxes. Economist don't like this kind of taxation – they prefer to let companies decide how many staff to employ rather than persuade them through taxes and subsidies. However, this narrow commercial decision fails to take into account the wider social benefits. If our policy aim is to maximise wellbeing through eliminating the human and social costs of unemployment, then some theoretical economic inefficiency is worth bearing.

The next challenge is to make sure that we don't break the labour market. In our example above, to raise an employee's wages by £1 would cost their employer £3; £1 of extra pay and £2 in reduced subsidies. This might make bosses think twice before offering a pay rise! This steep slope is called the 'withdrawal rate', and in another form it is one of the reasons why people get trapped on benefits in the first place. Currently if they take a low-paid job they can lose so much in benefits that it is hardly worth them working. Of course for employees it wouldn't be a problem, as they only see the actual difference in their pay packet. And for employers, the good news is that lower-paid jobs are very sensitive to pay rates. We have all seen stories of unions threatening industrial action over pay rises of around 2%, and people will consider changing jobs for 10% more. On £8 per hour that's 16p to make a fuss or 80p to make a move. So long as small changes can still create significant incentives, using pay rates to attract and retain staff remains viable.

Some people may have been out of work for so long that they have become almost incapable of holding down paid employment. There are certain personal and social skills needed for even the simplest job, like turning up on time and sober in the morning, following simple basic instructions, and getting through the day without abusing your customers or punching the boss. If workers do not possess even these most rudimentary life skills, their value to an employer is zero, and most would be unwilling to take them on even if they came for free. The answer is a combination of retraining and rehabilitation, with organisations paid for delivering these services and participants offered a basic salary for the duration of the programme. There are many excellent schemes in existence which have proved time and time again that it can be done. Most are delivered by community-based organisations rather than state or commercial enterprises. The problems that such individuals face go far deeper than a simple 'lack of skills' and, as we have seen, it is the community as an actor that possesses the greatest ability to tackle these more holistic and personal challenges.

The other main unskilled group in society are young people leaving school with few academic qualifications. For them, this approach offers a chance of meaningful trade apprenticeships, which used to be commonplace but are now either difficult to find or have become little more than a cover for low-paid work experience. By offsetting most of the costs of employing and training apprentices, we can both help the young people of today and plug the skills gaps of tomorrow.

Others will be reluctant to take the newly created jobs even if they are available. This can be for many reasons: fear of the unknown, low aspiration, lack of self-belief, simple laziness (yes, it does exist), or the fact that they will lose a lucrative 'double income' of state benefits and illegal cash-in-hand earnings. Some of the emotional and psychological issues can be helped by ready-for-work schemes as above. But it also has to be made impossible for people to remain on benefits by choice when work is available. The boldest decision would be to end unemployment benefits altogether once it has been proven that sufficient jobs exist. There would then be just two options: work; or training and preparation for work on a recognised scheme (which would have to be freely available to all). If it is felt that some kind of ultimate safety net has to be kept in place, then this must be time-limited,[27] and movement into work or preparation for work must be mandatory when offered.

Inwardly mobile

The benefits from this approach to ending the curse of unemployment should by now seem clear and obvious. But in the post-Brexit world, good ideas are not enough. We must be seen to be addressing the problems that led Britain to vote 'Leave' in the first place. And in the world of employment, that means tackling the issue of immigration. Would these changes help us to manage the number of people coming to the UK, and do they offer any protection to those most badly affected by international movement of people under the current arrangements?

The approach we have described would allow the market to solve both problems without any clumsy interventions involving quotas, caps, or visa restrictions. For lower-skilled positions (where large scale immigration is likely to lead directly to unemployment), there will be a massive incentive to employ local people. Why would you pay £8 per hour to hire a foreign worker when you could employ a local virtually for free? Even where locals may currently lack skills or experience, the economic benefits provide a powerful incentive to train them up. At the other end of the scale, for well paid and hard-to-fill skilled roles that are needed for companies to compete in a modern global economy, immigrants can be employed on equal terms and there would be no barrier to firms attracting the staff they need. In between these extremes, a smooth taper-off ensures that there are opportunities for progression and little risk of people becoming trapped in unskilled roles indefinitely.

Those economic migrants who continue to find employment under this system would do so because they brought much-needed skills and paid their own way. This at a stroke answers two of the key grievances which are often expressed: that immigrants either 'take our jobs' or 'live off our benefits system' (or paradoxically, get accused of both). As well as an efficient jobs market, there is an opportunity here to address one of the key causes of social division and community tension.

Up until now, the major barrier to implementing this approach would have been EU rules concerning free movement of people (and the automatic access to welfare and benefits that go with it). For the new system to work, it has to be restricted to citizens of our own nation. It operates by creating strong additional demand for low- to moderately-skilled workers, and this change to the balance of supply and demand means that there will always be enough jobs available for those who need them. If we allowed every unemployed person in Europe to access the same system, we would be back to where we started but with a massive additional burden on the UK taxpayer as we imported and subsidised low-skilled workers from across the continent.

Leaving the EU gives us a once-in-a-generation opportunity to move these ideas from economic theory to practical political reality. In negotiating Britain's future relationship with Europe, we do not have to withdraw completely from the idea of free movement of labour (a virtual political impossibility unless we also lose access to the single market and all the economic benefits that it brings). All we have to agree is the right to redesign our own social welfare system, from one which is based on providing cash benefits to the low-paid and unemployed (a major draw for economic migrants) to one which uses the market to guarantee the dignity of a job and a living wage for our own citizens while still allowing companies to draw on the international skills market as needed. Maybe in the area of employment of least, the rather fanciful 'policy on cake' adopted by the 'Leave' campaign ('pro having it and pro eating it')[28] may turn out to be viable after all.

Freedom of immobility

As we consider the current realities of the free movement of workers within Europe, we cannot help but notice a strange paradox. Why is it that so many relatively low-skilled roles in catering, hospitality, and other sectors are filled by migrant workers while large numbers of British people remain mired in long-term unemployment? When it is apparently easier for a young person from Lithuania to start a new life in London than for one from Liverpool to do the same, what we are experiencing is a crisis of mobility within the nation itself. Whenever there have been large changes in patterns of employment in the past, people have moved. The industrial revolution saw a massive shift of population away from rural communities to industrial towns and coalfields. The decline of heavy industry started to produce a similar trend of movement into new commercial centres, but during the past half-century this movement has largely ground to a halt. In all the arguments about freedom of movement within Europe, we seem to have lost sight of the fact that freedom of movement within the UK itself has been in decline for decades. Many of those who most urgently need the hope and opportunity that can come from finding a job are trapped in sprawling post-war social housing estates in areas of high unemployment, with little opportunity to break out and move. Freeing them from their situation is the issue we must turn to next.

4

TEAR DOWN THE SLUMS

It is not British civilisation that ails ... It is British council estates.

WILL HUTTON

Social housing has become the biggest benefits trap in post-war Britain.

SUNDER KATWALA

When we went out house-hunting back in 2001, we had a clear shopping list of features that we wanted to find. Our new home should be in the local area, have space for a growing family, my wife wanted some kind of studio space for her art, and I hoped for a real fire. After a great deal of searching and some careful financial calculations, the house we eventually bought fitted our list almost perfectly. My wife still laughs at me because the very first thing I did on moving in was to take a sledgehammer to the bricked-up fireplace and uncover a serviceable chimney behind. And today I am writing in the once-derelict workshop in the garden which we restored and turned into a peaceful art studio.

Our house-hunting story is no different to that which could be told by millions of other couples. We had dozens of factors we had to balance; some financial, some relational, some practical, some very personal to ourselves. Other factors we completely missed: our children were too young and our friends not middle-class enough for us to be worrying about secondary schools, but the fact that we turned out to have moved into the catchment area of a decent local comprehensive probably saved us from either a lot of travelling or having to move again.

The housing market provides a means for these millions of factors to be balanced and resolved. Prices in central London are extraordinarily high; a shorter commute can cost you literally thousands of pounds a minute. Space costs, as does proximity to good schools, nice scenery, decent leisure facilities or better employment prospects. What makes a 'good area' can be complex and intangible; things like crime statistics play a part, 'atmosphere' is easy to discern but hard to measure, and the appearance of the streets and houses themselves has a role to play. Most people could describe their ideal home in glowing and slightly unrealistic terms, but as always the ability of the market to discern the truth reveals the compromises they are actually willing to make. Will they opt for a small apartment in the heart of the city, or choose a big house further out but accept hours of travelling each day as the price of 'enjoying' it?

First choice

'Our' house was built in 1952 by the Shell oil company. Their rapidly expanding refinery at Shell Haven on the Thames estuary needed workers, and a lack of accommodation in the area was constraining their ability to attract suitable staff. Remarkably, in its 60-year history we were the first people ever to choose to live in the house through any kind of free and open process.

When they were first built, the homes on the Shell estate were allocated by the company through a kind of status-based paternalism. The main row of terraced houses on each block were given to process workers and tradesmen. The pair of semi-detached homes at the end of the row went to higher status occupations such as supervisors or foremen. Finally, on each of six prominent corners of the estate stood a four-bedroomed detached house with its own garage. These were reserved for professionals only; the house that we would eventually buy 50 years later was initially occupied by the company doctor. We don't know whether the doctor had a family or children to fill his spacious home but that wasn't the point; expectations in 1952 were still determined largely by class and status, and that was that.

By the 1960s the estate had passed to the management of the local council, and the refinery no longer had any direct control over who got to live there. Council houses were in theory allocated on the basis of need and your position on a waiting list (and if the rumours are to be believed, being related to a local councillor or having the right union connections could certainly help the process along too). Our predecessors originally came to live in the house via the council allocation route.

In the 1980s the government passed legislation granting a 'right to buy' to council tenants, meaning they could purchase their own home at a substantial discount. The scheme was controversial but extremely popular, especially for tenants living in well-built and spacious houses such as those on the Shell estate. The previous occupants of 'our' house took full advantage, and along with almost all of their neighbours became home-owners for the first time during that period.

As their children grew up and the owners reached retirement age, the garden started to feel like hard work and the roof on the workshop began to leak and cave in. Finally in 2001 they reached a decision, and sold the house to a young couple from the next town who were just starting out at the other end of family life. That couple was us, and we have called it home for more than a decade.

Residual value

While all this was going on, things down at the other end of our street were taking a slightly different path. Stanford-le-Hope and Corringham were still growing rapidly, and many of the new houses were being built directly by the local council. Unlike those from the 1950s, these 1960s and 1970s council estates were cheaply built, on smaller plots of land, included many more blocks of flats, and were radically designed with a complex maze of walkways that proved much less effective at forming functioning neighbourhoods than the more 'traditional' streets they were supposed to replace. Most people on the Shell estate had stable, relatively well-paid industrial jobs. These new estates tended to go to those who could not afford the private houses on the other side of town and, as the big industrial employers along the estuary started to lay off workers, they were joined by the ranks of the unemployed. Unsurprisingly right-to-buy proved less popular in these areas for anything other than the best houses.

By the time we bought our former council house in 2001, policy makers were starting to use the term 'residualised' to describe the flats and houses just a few hundred yards away at the other end of our street. A residue means the left-overs. These were the left-over houses; poorly built, on badly designed estates, plagued with crime and antisocial behaviour. And into them the system placed the people it regarded as 'left-over' too; those who had lost their jobs, single parents living through the aftermath of family break-up, and people on the lowest incomes. Those not able to make a wish-list as we had done, but forced to live wherever the council placed them.

As a local councillor I discovered first hand some of the problems that people experience on our two moderately sized council estates. But even by Thurrock standards these are by no means the worst. Elsewhere in our borough we have at least four estates which rank among the worst 10% of areas in the country for 'indexes of multiple deprivation'. If you live on one of these estates you are likely to experience the worst health, the lowest life expectancy, the poorest educational results, the greatest risk of family break-up, the worst crime rates, and the highest levels of unemployment of anyone in the UK. In other words, virtually every factor that affects your wellbeing will be going in the wrong direction. And, by national standards, Thurrock has it easy. Our pockets of deprivation are severe but localised. In some post-industrial towns and cities the pockets have merged to become large areas where entire generations are trapped without prospects and without hope.

The disaffection and anger that has taken root on Britain's council estates was one of the driving forces behind the vote to leave the EU. Because the votes were counted at district level, you can't produce an exact map that shows the relationship between social housing and the Brexit vote. The fact that Thurrock with its 10,000 council houses had one of the highest 'Leave' percentages in the country is certainly indicative. But for hard evidence you need look no further than the growth of the UKIP vote on these estates, year after year. Some Thurrock wards on post-war council estates have gone from 'safe Labour' to 'safe UKIP' within a single electoral cycle. These voters are not driven by slightly abstract debates about sovereignty and EU bureaucracy. Private polling in the run-up to the 2015 general election showed that Britain's membership of the EU was (astonishingly) only the sixth most important issue for likely UKIP voters. Number one was immigration, followed by a raft of issues which the 'Leave' campaign was able to link successfully to immigration: jobs, housing, public services, and the economy. These are the actual issues that were affecting people's lives, and they were hungry for change. The surveys showed that people knew the EU itself wasn't the heart of the problem, but getting out was the only opportunity for dramatic change they had been given in a decade. When the chance was offered, Britain's council estates seized it with both hands.

Inside the trap

How can it be that where you live can have such an enormous effect on your prospects in life? And if the location of the 'worst' estates is common knowledge, why do people still choose to live there anyway?

The initial reason is financial. For all its failings, social housing[29] has one big advantage: it comes with a massive government subsidy. To rent a one-bedroomed flat in Thurrock you would expect to pay around £130 per week.[30] A council flat will cost you just over £80; fully a third less. If you want a three-bedroomed family home the difference is even greater: a council house (if you can get one) will cost you just over £100 per week, compared to at least £200 for a private rental. This is half-price accommodation.

On one Thurrock council estate there was a joke doing the rounds: 'How do you tell the difference between a council house and a private rental? The council house has a new BMW on the drive.' And indeed, if two households are earning the same income but one is in a council property and the others are private tenants, their difference in disposable income will be about £400 a month; easily enough to cover the payments on a new car (or a family holiday, designer label clothes, consumer gadgets, or whatever).

Once you are in a council property the financial benefits are yours for life. It is about the only form of state welfare which is granted based on need but then continues for ever regardless of need. To be allocated a council house you have to meet strict criteria. You must be on low income or state benefits, not have significant financial savings, and either wait your turn on the list or demonstrate some form of urgent housing need such as medical requirements, homelessness, or overcrowding. However, if your salary then increases, you come into a large sum of money, or the special circumstances which created your need change significantly, your right to remain in that council house is unaffected. But if you ever decide to take the risk of moving on, it is gone for ever. Not only will you go to the end of the queue, there is a good chance that you may not get back on the list at all.

The jaws of the trap are now sprung. For anyone in difficult financial circumstances, the low cost of social housing makes it an attractive lifeline. Once in, you have every incentive to stay put. For many the 'holy grail' of social housing is a family sized home in a decent area away from the roughest estates (maybe like one of the few council houses that still remain on the Shell estate). Every year you spend in that high-rise council block puts you a little higher up the waiting list and maybe a year closer towards fulfilling that dream. But at the same time, it makes it harder and harder to try and do something to improve your own situation. The idea of taking on a bigger rent or a mortgage to move somewhere else is scary enough as it is. If it also means that you lose your place on the council waiting list, then it may seem like a risk not worth taking.

Much safer to stay where you are and spend the money on council rent and lottery scratchcards. People are spending their entire lives in surroundings that kill hope and destroy aspiration, trapped by fear of the unknown and the slim chance that tomorrow they may get given a ticket out.

In fact, the chance of you ever reaching that elusive peak of the social housing ladder is getting almost as unlikely as a lottery win. Firstly, those who are currently in those houses are not going anywhere. If you have waited half your life for the best council house in the area and are now living in it at half the market rent, where is your incentive to move on? The fact that you were given the house in the first place because you had four teenage children who have now left home is irrelevant; possession is ten-tenths of the law.[31] Secondly, there are a whole range of scams available to help someone more ruthless than you get to the front of the queue. Because housing is allocated on the basis of need and some needs are considered more urgent than others, a perverse incentive is created for people to allow their circumstances to become worse rather than better. In any other area of life this would carry its own penalties. In the world of social housing, self-improvement is penalised while getting deeper into trouble is rewarded. Here, from personal experience, are some tried and tested ways of getting ahead in the social housing race-to-the-bottom (and there are plenty of others):

1. Start living with your boyfriend/girlfriend. Then split up. One of you is now 'homeless' and automatically entitled to be re-housed. The worse you have treated each other, the more convincing the break-up and the better your chances.

2. Get your parents to throw you out of the house. If you have to get involved in drugs or violence, then so be it. So long as you can convince the housing office that the situation is genuine, you can move straight into your own place.

3. Find a new partner with children of their own from a previous relationship, and invite them to move in with you.

You are now overcrowded, and entitled to an urgent move to a bigger place. Now split up again. You will probably get to keep the larger property, and the other person will be re-housed anyway.

4. Get a job. Get a flat. Don't be too enthusiastic about paying the rent on time. Lose the job. Your landlord will give you a letter saying that you have to leave at the end of your tenancy. Take the letter to the housing office. Job done.

5. Get pregnant. It's such a cliché and the tabloids hate it, but it still works and sometimes the old ideas are the best.

Of course, the vast majority of people are not deliberately indulging it tactics like this. But that honest majority are losing out, and they know it. It brings the system into disrepute, it stigmatises council tenants as 'scroungers', and it creates a climate of moral hazard where bad choices are rewarded. So when circumstances get tough, where is the incentive to solve your own problems and play by the rules? And every one of these things that the system encourages (broken relationships, unemployment, social isolation) is proven to damage wellbeing.

In this short journey we have seen how a mindset can be shifted from one where no-one in their right mind would want to live on the worst council estates, to one where people will fight and cheat for the chance to do exactly that. And when all of your hopes are riding on getting a council house, you become hyper-sensitive to the issue of immigration. Every home that is allocated to a foreigner means that you or your children drop one place further down the list. That person from the EU or elsewhere isn't just competing with you in the labour market in some abstract sense, they have now moved into the council house which you applied for or desperately wanted and have to walk past every day. It's hard to imagine a scenario more calculated to stir up resentment and racial tension. As a society we have built the system that created this mess, and we have the responsibility to dismantle it. So where do we begin?

The great escape

A decent quality home, in a functioning community and a safe and secure environment, is one of the most fundamental drivers of wellbeing that there is. Millions lack these things for two simple reasons: property in the UK is too expensive, and attempts to offer a more affordable alternative in the form of 'social housing' have too often proved a disastrous failure. We will need to come at this problem from both ends, but let's start with the social housing issue.

No-one would ever build a road that runs straight up a cliff face. Instead the designers use a combination of tunnels, cuttings, embankments, and alternative routes to make the gradient shallow enough for vehicles to negotiate. The same is true for markets. Where there is a steady gradient of price and quality, people's choices make a difference and they can choose to spend a little more in return for an extra room or the chance to live in a more desirable area (whatever that means for them). But at the moment, social housing behaves more like a cliff edge. The jump from a council rent of £400 per month to a private rent of £800 is so huge that it feels almost impossible to cross from one to the other. The people living on our 'bottom 10%' housing estates are effectively stuck there because a whole section of the market which should allow them to climb their way out simply doesn't exist. What looked like a lifeline at a time of crisis rapidly turns out to be a one way ticket to deprivation.

It may sound like the problem is a financial one, and that private rents are 'too expensive' compared to social rents, but this isn't quite true. Speak to anyone involved in finance, and they will tell you that the value of an asset (money in the bank, stocks and shares, or a rental flat in Thurrock) is interchangeable with the income you can make from holding it. So £80,000 in the bank might pay me £150 per month in interest (not much, but at least it's fairly safe).[32] £80,000 invested in the stock market might make £500 per month in dividends and growth (but the stock market could crash again in which case my gains could turn into a loss). £80,000 invested in a flat should also generate £500 per month in rental income (although I will have to pay maintenance costs and agent's fees out of that). Which I choose will depend on the returns on offer and how much risk I am willing to accept, but the point is that the 'value' of my asset is effectively equal to what I will receive by owning it.

Thurrock Council owns a lot of flats. It rents them out for something over £300 per month, well below the £500 that it could get if it simply advertised them in a local estate agent's window. That difference of £200 is real money; it is the difference between the value that the asset should be able to generate for its owner (the taxpayer) and what they are actually making from it. It is the hidden subsidy paid to anyone who is allocated social housing. It is the cause of the 'cliff edge', and for larger properties it is even bigger, meaning that families are at even greater risk of being trapped.

For someone living entirely on state benefits (who might be unemployed but could equally be a pensioner), the state is already paying them the full £500 cost of their flat. £300 goes to them directly in the form of housing benefit payments, which they then pay back to the council as rent. The other £200 remains hidden; it is the difference between what the flat is 'worth' as an asset and what the council actually charges for it. So to say that there is not enough money to pay market rates for social housing is not actually true. The state is already paying the full market price to house every welfare recipient; it just does so in a roundabout way where some of the amount is visible but some remains hidden.

The first part of the answer should now be becoming obvious. Let's say that tomorrow we increase the housing related element of benefit payments being made to everyone living on welfare in a one-bedroomed flat in Thurrock from £300 to £500. At the same time, the council increases the rent it charges on these properties to the full market value, also around £500. No-one's financial position has changed at all. The tenant is still receiving benefit payments which fully cover their rent, so they can still afford to live. The state is still paying out the same amount in benefits as it gets back in rent, so there is no greater demand on the public finances. But now the cliff edge is gone. Instead of being trapped in a sink estate, the tenant can now choose to move if they wish. Maybe they will go closer to a job, a school, or a family member who can offer them some support. Maybe they will choose to live somewhere smaller but in an area with less crime and antisocial behaviour. Previously the size of property they were allocated was decided by a bureaucrat based on theoretical need, but now they are free to make the same choices and tradeoffs that my wife and I and almost everyone else in society makes whenever they decide to move house.

The domino effect

Implementing this policy should be simple because it will be extremely popular. No matter how many times the BBC explains that it won't make anyone a penny better off, people who are getting a whole load of extra money in their pocket are going to feel a lot richer and more empowered. In fact the only losers will be those who are still living in social housing despite now being on average or above-average incomes. Their rents will rise, but because they are not welfare recipients there will be no corresponding increase in benefit payments. Clearly there will need to be transitional cushioning arrangements, but it is already widely accepted as unfair that a small section of society continues to receive a lifetime cash subsidy in the form of a council house that they would no longer qualify for if they applied again today.

Some form of means-tested welfare system will need to remain, to ensure that people on low incomes can afford an acceptable standard of housing. Even after the employment reforms suggested in the previous chapter, there will still be people living on low wages of around £10 per hour. This is sufficient for a single person living alone, and these changes free them up to make the kind of housing choices that most of us already take for granted. Choices such as: will I spend a large proportion of my income on rent as the price of independence, or will I choose to stay living with friends or family and keep my costs down? Suddenly good choices are rewarded and bad ones come at a cost, rather than the other way round. But for someone trying to support a family this income would be totally inadequate. If we do not wish to see children living in poverty, then some form of assistance to cover the higher costs of housing a family (and feeding and clothing them) will be necessary. The housing component of this should reflect the principles already described: it should be paid direct to the individual, at local rates, and allow them to make their own choices in the local housing market.[33]

That market itself will start to experience significant changes. The few remaining council houses on the part of our street originally built by Shell will be attractive places to live, and market rents will remain comfortably above the local average. On some of the worst housing estates elsewhere in Thurrock, rental values are likely to collapse. Why would you choose to continue living somewhere with so many problems when you have now been empowered to make your own choices? The market will do what it does best; it will resolve the complexity of matching everyone's wants, needs, and preferences to the range of housing available, and it will expose the truth of what some of these estates are really worth. For some of them the answer may be that they are near worthless. This will unlock the opportunity for investment and refurbishment, or demolition and redevelopment. For others the rents may stabilise at a lower level. This means that those who choose to remain will enjoy a significantly higher disposable income, or a larger property to live in, or both. For some people this will feel like an attractive deal (that's the whole point of how markets determine prices; the buyer must feel they are happy or they won't sign up). The psychological effect on those communities will be massive. In a few years time, no-one will be living there other than by choice (albeit still a difficult and constrained choice in some cases). The physical environment may not change overnight, but the conditions for hope, aspiration, and growing community relationships will be restored. This has to have a positive effect on wellbeing in the long term.

The current providers of social housing will undergo a significant upheaval. Local councils, housing associations, arms-length management organisations, and registered social landlords (the various bodies with legal rights and obligations to provide subsidised housing in the UK) will experience a change of purpose. Instead of providing and rationing out housing at below-market rates as at present, their new role will be to provide decent quality, reasonably priced homes at the lower end of the open market. This remains a valuable and worthwhile objective. Private landlords do not always enjoy the best of reputations, and the presence of not-for-profit organisations driven by a social purpose will be invaluable in setting market standards and preventing a 'race to the bottom'. The financial value of their asset base will rise, because the value of the rental income it produces will significantly increase. Most of this gain is needed to fund the increase in welfare payments which in turn pays those rents. Arrangements will have to be put in place to ensure that the finances balance and neither the state, individuals, nor the housing organisations become winners or losers as a result.[34] Where properties are still in state ownership, decisions will have to be made over the longer term whether these assets are to be retained or sold.[35]

One of the greatest disappointments of the post-war social housing dream has been the failure to nurture functioning communities. The designers of the first tower blocks saw them as 'streets in the sky' into which thriving neighbourhoods could be transplanted. The grim reality has been the exact opposite of this. But just as an overbearing state and market tend to suppress community, this combination of a reformed market and less intrusive state can provide opportunities for community to grow and thrive. The problems of the worst housing estates are multifaceted and deeply ingrained. Ending the social housing trap removes one of the most powerful root causes, but the complex range of human, social, cultural, and spiritual damage which needs to be repaired is the kind of task that only the community can undertake. Community is organic in its nature; you can't make it happen but you can prepare the ground, pull up the weeds, and nurture what starts to emerge. This type of community regeneration must go hand in hand with the more physical kind.

At the same time, the new freedoms which are created should support the strengthening of relationships as one of the key pillars of wellbeing. The current system actively encourages the fragmentation of family units. In principle, the tough choice to remain together is a sound one in both human and financial terms. We must encourage these kinds of choices to be made and supported in practice. Beyond the immediate family unit, numerous examples of community living continue to emerge if you know where to look, often inspired by shared spiritual or environmental goals and actively promoting wider community relationships. You do not need to agree with all of their beliefs to recognise that they are financially efficient, environmentally sound, and relationally potent. All of these traits are positive for wellbeing, and it is clear that we do not in any case have sufficient housing available for the trend towards fragmented living to continue. With the social housing trap removed, a freedom for people to experiment with alternative models of community is something which can be actively supported.

A price worth paying?

Although the housing market has strengths that we can and should put to work, it also clearly has some serious limitations. Try explaining the virtues of a free market to the family struggling to keep up their mortgage payments or the young couple who find even the most modest property is beyond their reach, and they may take some convincing. The bottom line is that the average price of a house in Britain is around six times average income.[36] That is simply unaffordable unless you have some alternative source of finance available.

The problem, as always with markets, is one of supply and demand. Britain is a small island with a large population and limited supplies of land available for building. Even if it were not, the reality is that the 'demand' for a better house in a nicer location seems to be almost unlimited. Maybe we should not be surprised at this. The ONS happiness survey showed that owning your own home correlates directly with higher wellbeing.[37] When something relates so directly to such a deeply felt human need, it is perhaps inevitable that demand will remain strong regardless of price. However, the supply situation is certainly not helping. We have created a planning system that makes developers and landowners rich, makes homebuyers poor, has failed to produce new homes in anywhere near the quantities needed, yet has made communities feel powerless to influence development that seems to happen without their involvement or consent. We will come back to this point later.

The other main driver in the housing market is the availability of money. We all know that 'cheap' money drives up house prices; this was one of the main causes of the 2008 financial crash. Borrowing became so easy that house prices were inflated well beyond sustainable levels, and when the situation finally flipped it brought entire banks and economies crashing down with it. But even in more sober economic times, home ownership remains at the very limit of affordability for the majority of people in the UK.

The only people who can now afford to buy property are high earners, those who got onto the housing ladder before prices took off, or recipients of inherited wealth. Given the financial benefits that come from owning your home rather than paying rent to a landlord, the last category is particularly worrying. Imagine two people buying identical houses in a typical UK street. One is able to pay cash, using money inherited from their family. The other takes out a mortgage which they intend to repay over 25 years. By the end of the term both will own their houses, but the effects of compound interest mean that the second buyer will have paid twice as much as the first.[38] If this situation is allowed to continue, we will be back to a society where the rich get richer, the poor get poorer, and this divide passes on from generation to generation. Any concept of fairness or merit will be replaced by the grim reality of Disraeli's two nations, hardwired into the housing market.

The interaction between financial markets and house prices has already brought the world to the brink of ruin and left millions of people either homeless or burdened by unaffordable debt. To suggest that our objective should now be to return things 'back to normal' seems pretty naïve given what happened before and could presumably happen again. But so far, no-one seems to be able to come up with any better ideas. The search for a financial system which is able to harness the strength of markets without falling victim to their evident flaws will now take us on a compelling journey into the very nature of money itself.

5

SEIZE THE MONEY SUPPLY

Money, being in itself naturally barren, it is preposterous to make it breed more money.

ARISTOTLE

Faced by failure of credit they have proposed only the lending of more money.

FRANKLIN D. ROOSEVELT

The wintry sun was already getting low in the sky as the big Mercedes estate left Thurrock and pushed deeper into the Essex countryside. As you head northwards, the roads and villages become smaller and the properties get bigger. Our destination was a large house standing by itself on a secluded country lane, surrounded by what looked suspiciously like a moat. Here I had been promised that I would be introduced to a man who could finally explain to me exactly where money comes from.

My quest to locate the source of money had started about a year earlier, when I had come across a group of Christian monetary justice campaigners who were claiming that almost all of the money in circulation is created out of thin air by banks. Having pulled off this rather neat trick, the banks then add insult to injury by charging us interest to use the stuff. Some of their ideas sounded crazy, and to be honest I couldn't believe that the situation was quite as simple or stark as they were making out.[39] But it bugged me that I couldn't provide any better explanations. They at least had researched their subject, whereas I and everyone else I knew were just carrying on earning, borrowing, and spending the stuff with no real idea of where it came from or what effect our actions were having. None of us realised back then that the great financial crash of 2008 was just five years away, but even in an environment of what seemed like endless growth and stability it was un-nerving that something as important as money became so difficult to understand the closer you examined it.

Fortunately we had a close friend who was a retired director in a major high street bank. I asked him about it and he confirmed that banks do 'sort of' create money themselves. Ever the practical engineer, I asked if he could show me the room where they actually did it. Somewhere about this point he admitted that his knowledge was pretty much exhausted. His background was in investment banking, but he did have a former colleague who had specialised in lending and was now serving as an adviser to the Bank of England on financial markets. I was slightly nervous that my ignorant questions were going to make both me and my friend look stupid, but he assured me that it would be OK and a visit to meet the colleague at his home was arranged.

He certainly knew his stuff, and duly provided about the most helpful and comprehensive explanation of the money supply I have ever heard in one place. Some of my questions must have seemed a bit naïve, but having taken the precaution of swotting up some economics beforehand I did just about have the vocabulary to understand the answers I was getting. That trip into the Essex countryside provided the last missing pieces of the jigsaw, and the picture which emerged has continued to surprise and provoke me ever since.

Blame the bankers

Fast forward just a couple of years, and suddenly everyone was interested in money. Not where it came from, but where it had all gone. The financial crisis which started in 2008 cost the global economy over $10 trillion. Or maybe $20 trillion. No-one really seems to know. Numbers like this are impossible to comprehend. It would pay for the financial costs of the worst natural or man-made disasters (like the Boxing Day tsunami or the 9/11 terrorist attacks) five hundred times over. Imagine a 9/11 in every capital city on earth followed by 200 tsunamis. If you suggested that as a plot for a disaster movie you would be laughed out of Hollywood.

The causes and immediate effects of the crisis were concentrated in a handful of massive global banks, but the fallout hit ordinary people hard. Homes were repossessed, jobs lost, wages frozen for years, pensions decimated, and businesses destroyed. As governments committed billions of taxpayers' money to sorting out the mess, there was a real sense that those responsible for causing the problem had escaped any form of justice. Bankers got bailouts while everyone else got austerity. Even though none of those protesting could offer any better ideas, the effect on trust in governments and 'the system' was profound. People looked at the actions of Britain and the EU and concluded that either their political leaders were in cahoots with the ultra-wealthy, or they were powerless to stand up to them. Neither is acceptable in a democracy.

This anti-establishment mood was one of the key themes of the Brexit campaign. When people looked at Europe, they didn't see a club whose members enjoyed economic stability and prosperity. They saw unemployment, sovereign debt crises, profligate Greeks, corrupt Italians, and unyielding Germans. Referendum voters were told that EU membership was vital for Britain's continued access to the global financial system, and concluded that they wanted no further part of it.

I have a good degree of sympathy for the politicians who found themselves responding to a crisis on an unprecedented scale with no obvious right answers. Their willingness to take unpopular decisions probably prevented a complete financial meltdown and for that they deserve more credit than they are often given. But performing costly emergency repairs on an overheating car after the engine has blown up does not mean that everything will then be OK. It's almost certainly time for a new car. Leaving the EU could yet plunge Britain's financial services sector into further crisis. But it could also represent a huge opportunity, not just to add some additional checks and balances but to completely re-think how we manage the money supply for the wellbeing of all. And that brings us right back to the original question: where does money come from, and is it time for a change?

A brief history of money

In the beginning, people used to swap sheep for stuff. Sheep have some obvious limitations as a currency; not everyone will always accept them, they are difficult to fit in your pocket, they are hard to store for long periods, and it's even harder to give change (unless you are doing a deal with the butcher). What was needed was a currency that was easy to use, difficult to fake, and kept its value well over time. The first widely accepted form of money was precious metals such as silver or gold, which have been in use for several thousand years.[40] Greek and Roman rulers issued gold and silver coins bearing their own imprint, partly as a means of quality control and to avoid the need to weigh them out every time, and partly to assert their control over economic life.

Gold coins can be bulky to handle when used in large quantities, and are also vulnerable to theft. Medieval goldsmiths would store gold on their customers behalf and issue 'notes' to prove their ownership. These notes were actually easier to use than the gold itself for large transactions, and the idea of paper money was born. As this type of money grew in importance, the issue of bank notes was gradually taken over by governments. Somewhere around the same time the practice of lending out someone else's gold to merchants for a period in return for a share of their profits became commonplace, and goldsmiths took the first step on the journey to becoming modern lending banks.

Up until the 1930s all paper money was still ultimately backed by gold. The wording on a British bank note that said 'I promise to pay the bearer on demand the sum of one pound' meant exactly that. In theory, you could go to the Bank of England and demand the fixed quantity of gold that your bank note represented. It was the pressures of war and the rapid expansion of global trade that eventually made this system too slow and inflexible to regulate the international money system. The gold standard and countries' departure from it played a big role in the great depression of the 1930s, and was largely concluded when the US dollar broke the final connection to gold in 1971. Since then, the promise on every bank note has been backed not by gold but by the nation itself. Ultimately the promise to make good on your otherwise valueless paper note will be funded through future trade, taxation, and economic production. All the while that you and I and everyone else believe that this promise is credible, the money continues to have value and we all carry on using and accepting it. This type of money is known as *fiat* currency, from a Latin word which means 'let it be so'.

Even before governments broke the final links with gold in the twentieth century, banks had discovered that they could be made 'flexible' in practice. Because you could issue a loan in the form of a note rather than lending out the physical gold itself, there was nothing in theory to stop you lending out more money than you actually had on deposit. So long as everyone repaid their loans and your depositors never all came asking for their money back at the same time, lending out more than you had on deposit seemed harmless – and highly profitable. Why just charge interest once, when you could issue more loans and collect interest on two, three, or four times the amount of money that you actually had in your vaults? Both you and your wealthy investors would do extremely well out of the arrangement, and the borrowers were not complaining either. They now had access to funds which enabled them to build the industrial, commercial, and military empires of the eighteenth and nineteenth centuries. Many of these ventures proved extremely lucrative, and although a few inevitably went bust, the profits flowing back in proved more than adequate to keep repaying the loans and piling up the interest.

Show me the room where it happens

This quick overview is the one you will find in any economics textbook, and most people choose to end their journey there.

But it does leave some obvious unanswered questions. Where do banks actually get the physical money to lend out, when their total lending already exceeds the amount of currency printed by the government? If we can't answer this question then the accusation from the monetary justice campaigners that they create it out of thin air is starting to look justified.

Imagine that I go to my bank on Friday and ask to borrow £100 to get me through to the end of the month. They put the money into my account and I go out and spend it on new tyres for my car. I pay by card, and the money goes straight out of my bank account and into the garage's account. Because it is Friday, the garage pays the £100 to one of their tyre-fitters as part of a weekly wage, which goes straight into his bank. After work he goes down to Lakeside shopping centre and blows the whole lot on a new mobile phone he has had his eye on. The mobile phone shop pays £50 to the network provider as part of the deal, and spends the other £50 settling a bill with the company who came to install their window displays last week.

By the end of the working day the £100 I borrowed has already moved on three times and is now sitting in two other bank accounts; one belonging to the mobile phone network and the other to the window display company. But the point is, it is still there in a bank account somewhere. If they both use the same bank as me, then by the end of the day the total amount of loans and deposits in all the various accounts will exactly balance out. If they happen to use a different bank then my bank will have to go to it and borrow the money overnight to make their books balance, which they do through a process known as 'clearing'. In the old days all these transactions would have been recorded in paper ledgers and may well have involved cash. Today it happens almost instantly through bank cards and computer systems, but the principle is still the same.

Where did the money come from to fund the loan for my new tyres? The money came into existence at the moment I agreed to borrow it, and as I passed it on to someone else, they became richer by exactly the amount required to lend it back to me in the first place. Did the bank create the loan out of thin air? At the point that they made me the loan then the answer is 'yes', but they did so in the certain knowledge that the money would flow off round the system and in the end someone would deposit it back with them (or another bank). This deposit would exactly cover the value of the original loan, and it always does because while money moves from place to place, it never disappears.[41] Was there a physical room where it happened? Certainly not one that you can point to. Money is created all the time, whenever I use a credit card, borrow on an overdraft, or take out a loan. The system handles this as effortlessly as blowing up a balloon; it just gets bigger as more air is forced in.

Banks cannot keep lending indefinitely; the rules require that they hold a certain amount of money back as 'capital reserves' for unforeseen circumstances (like someone going bankrupt and failing to pay back their loan). Current regulations put this figure at up to 10%.[42] So if a bank starts with £1,000 in hard cash or other assets, that means that it can lend out up to £900, keeping the rest back as a reserve. But as we have seen, all that lending will immediately appear back in the banking system as new deposits. This £900 of 'new' deposits can be lent out too, so long as they hold onto £90 as their 10% capital reserve. The £810 again comes back round the system as new deposits, and £729 is available for further loans. We have now lent over £2,400 based on our original £1,000, and the money is still flowing. If you follow the chain to its end you will find that up to £10,000 can be lent out based on our original £1.000, still nominally maintaining an ample 10% capital reserve.

It is thus hardly surprising that 95% of the money in circulation today is created in this way. We use money for three basic purposes: as a convenient means of exchange to enable buying and selling to take place; as a means of allocating and distributing the material goods (both necessities and luxuries) that money can buy; and as a store of wealth that can be spent in the future. All are essential for any modern society to operate. Commercial banks have established an almost complete monopoly on managing this money supply on behalf of the nation. In many ways it is like a private utility. The banks create enough money for the economy to keep flowing and to govern and manage the allocation of labour, capital assets, and natural resources, both now and into the future. For doing this they charge interest; some gets paid to depositors and the rest they keep for themselves as profit. It may only be a few percentage points, but it has two important effects. Firstly the system will keep growing indefinitely, because if 95% of the money in existence must eventually be paid back with interest then even more money will be needed next year to cover the total. And secondly, as we saw with our example of the two house buyers, even the necessities of life come with an interest charge attached to them and this guarantees a permanent flow of wealth from the 'have-nots' into the pockets of the 'haves'.

Losing interest

Interest payments have been regarded with a degree of moral suspicion from the moment they were invented. When Moses gave the ten commandments, they came with an appendix that included a specific law against charging interest on loans.[43] Further biblical passages expand on the evils of interest, and similar laws are also found in the Qur'an. The challenge is not just an abstract theological one. In the year 2000, over $100 billion of debts for some of the poorest third-world countries were cancelled after sustained pressure from the 'Jubilee Debt Campaign', an international coalition in which Christian and other religious groups featured heavily.[44]

In the Middle Ages, Christians, Jews, and Muslims all had laws preventing money-lending at interest. However, the pressure to finance wars or commercial ventures was steadily growing and borrowing was seen as one of the obvious solutions. The first to find a way round the religious authorities were the Jewish bankers. Their Rabbis forbade lending at interest to fellow Jews, but allowed such loans to be made to Gentiles (i.e. everyone else). Christians at the time were not allowed to charge interest to anyone, so Jewish businessmen were able to make their fortunes in banking because they were the only people who could legally lend money to the expanding European merchant classes. It is no coincidence that the moneylender Shylock in Shakespeare's 'The Merchant of Venice' (*c.* 1597) was portrayed as a Jew.

The merchants of Christian Europe (including Venice) were not going to take this lying down, and the scheme their lawyers came up with was called the *contractum trinius*. This created a set of three contracts (an interest-free loan, an insurance policy, and a right for the borrower to keep any profits made over and above an agreed amount). Each was entirely legal under church law, but together they had exactly the same effect as a loan at a fixed rate of interest. The church authorities were powerless to stop the *contractum trinius*, and laws against interest gradually faded away in Christian countries.[45] Most Christians do still consider that the Bible condemns excessive interest, especially when levied on the poor and vulnerable, hence their leading role in the Jubilee Debt Campaign.

Jewish bankers were still unable to lend to other religious Jews, and this led to the invention of the *heter iska*. This converts the loan arrangement into an investment partnership between the two parties, one of whom brings the money to the table and the other their time and business skills. The 'money' investor effectively makes their return by claiming a share of the profits. The idea is that both risks and rewards are shared, although the deal can be structured to make it work similarly to a conventional interest-bearing loan in practice.

Modern Islamic banking has grown rapidly with the emergence of oil-rich and increasingly developed Muslim countries. Islamic banks again do not charge interest in the strict sense of the term, but use arrangements such as *mudarabah* (an investment partnership similar to the Jewish *heter iska*) or *murabaha* (a form of hire-purchase where the final price paid for an item by the borrower is greater than that originally paid out by the lender).

There are probably three things we can learn from the complex and at times confrontational relationship between religion and finance. Firstly, there are genuine moral concerns that interest can become a means for exploiting the vulnerable and transferring wealth from the poor to the rich. Secondly, that more ethically satisfactory arrangements such as joint ventures and risk/reward sharing do exist. And finally, that no laws and regulations can prevent the charging of interest if the parties are determined to get round them. Interest-bearing loans can certainly sometimes be exploitative, but they are also often useful and can bring advantages to all those involved.

Power to the people

We have seen that creating and regulating the money supply has become a form of private utility. It is a vastly complex enterprise, and one which no modern economy can manage without. Yet through its reliance on credit interest as the primary fiscal control mechanism, it runs a real risk of generating and perpetuating inequality and thus fundamentally damaging wellbeing. It is also potentially unstable, as the 2008 'credit crunch' and its aftermath amply demonstrate.

There is another utility that is essential to modern society and that has to handle complex and variable demands at the moment that they become apparent. That utility is the supply of electricity. At the end of this paragraph I am going to walk to the kitchen and switch the kettle on. No-one can predict exactly when I am going to do it, and my kettle will instantly require about two kilowatts (the output of a small petrol generator) to make me a cup of tea. Yet I fully expect that the national grid will somehow manage to produce the extra power that I need without any adverse affects at all.

Five minutes later my tea is made, and as expected the brief surge in demand was met without a hitch. Many of us never bother to stop and think about exactly how this is achieved, but as a former power station engineer I know that there are three different types of power plant involved. They all play different and complementary roles in keeping the system stable and matching demand to supply.

One of the first power stations I trained at was Oldbury, a nuclear plant on the Severn estuary not far from Bristol. Oldbury was what is known as a 'base load' generator. It relied on the fact that although demand for electricity varies throughout the day, it never normally falls below a certain minimum value. Day and night we kept on producing the same amount of electricity, often for months at a time.

Despite the fact that nuclear power is seen by many people as fraught with danger, life at Oldbury was generally safe and reassuringly dull. Sometimes the only thing of any interest to happen on an entire eight-hour shift was that the tour guides would come round with a group of visitors wanting to see inside the control room. The guide would knock on the doors, have a brief word with the Charge Engineer, then tell the visitors that they were in luck and would be able to go in in a few minutes. This suitably built up the suspense, while giving us enough time to prepare. Preparation involved getting rid of the foreman's bike, hiding the tea trolley round the back of the reactor control cabinets, removing any stray copies of the *Sun* or *Daily Mail* from the control desks, and everyone putting on a white coat to present the appropriate air of calm scientific professionalism.

If life at Oldbury was pretty predictable, my first 'real' job at West Thurrock power station on the Thames estuary was anything but. West Thurrock was a 'load following' station, whose output varied throughout the course of the day to meet the ever-changing demand for power. In the UK, demand for electricity is at its lowest overnight, and rises steeply in the morning as shops, offices, factories and schools all start their working day. It fluctuates a little throughout the day, and in winter it normally hits a peak around 5pm as all the lights go on and the demands of commercial and domestic consumers overlap during the travel home period. Things then drop off again ready for the overnight lull.

At West Thurrock we could expect to shut down overnight then run up quickly over a couple of hours in the morning as demand picked up. During the day our generators would be set to automatic, constantly adjusting their output to meet the fluctuating demand for power. As the evening peak arrived we would often get the call telling us to go to 'max gen', which meant giving them every megawatt we could manage to squeeze out of the aging turbines.

Constantly starting up and shutting down puts strains on the plant, so things at West Thurrock tended to break a lot more frequently than they did at Oldbury. Running at less than full output for much of the day also made our power more expensive. But we did provide a valuable service in matching supply to demand, and thus ensuring that people could switch on their kettles whenever they liked without causing a power cut further down the street.

The third and most intriguing power plant of all was Dinorwig, in the mountains of North Wales. I never worked at Dinorwig, but did do a stint at the National Grid control centre from where it is remotely operated. Dinorwig is a 'peak load' station which uses a technology called pumped storage. Overnight, gigantic pumps deep inside a man-made cavern move up to a million tons of water from a lake in an old slate quarry to a reservoir near the top of the mountain above. During the day the pumps are reversed to act as generators, and sit waiting for the signal to come. When it does, Dinorwig can go from zero to full load in just over ten seconds (the time it takes the water to get from the top of the mountain to the bottom), and instantly be equalling the entire output of a large fossil-fuelled or nuclear power station.

Dinorwig does not actually 'produce' any electricity at all. Because you always have to put in more power in pumping mode than you get back out in generator mode, it actually absorbs about a third more power than it generates. But it comes into its own for managing sudden surges in demand, and the most common reason for these is our collective enthusiasm for watching television. At the end of a TV programme I will often get up from my chair, switch on the kettle, and make a cup of tea (rather like I did earlier). The trouble is, everyone else who was watching the same programme may well be having the same idea. Even a normal episode of a popular soap opera will cause a power surge equal to a hundred thousand kettles all being turned on at once. The highest incidence of 'TV pickup' ever recorded in the UK was at the end of the penalty shootout between England and Germany in the semi-final of the 1990 World Cup. England lost 4–3 on penalties, and after an experience like that the English really need a good strong cup of tea. The demand for electricity surged by over a million kettles[46] within the space of a few minutes. Luckily the grid control centre were watching TV too (for professional reasons, obviously) and, with the help of Dinorwig, managed to ensure the lights stayed on.

One trick pony

The similarities between the management of the money supply and the electricity supply are obvious. The demand for money comes in different forms, from the long-term stable (like domestic mortgages or borrowing on large capital projects which are paid back predictably over decades), through the day-to-day movements of the finance markets, to sudden 'shocks' like the 1929 Wall Street crash or the 2008 banking collapse. Money also comes at a cost; as we have seen, 95% of the money in circulation is created with interest attached as the cost of using it.

But unlike electricity, our current means of managing the money supply depends almost entirely on a single source. Almost all of the money we use comes from commercial banks where it is created as interest-bearing loans. It is as if we were trying to meet the entire demand of the economy using West Thurrock style financial power stations. They can do the job of day-to-day load following, but are an expensive way to provide steady, predictable base-load supplies and also lack the speed and flexibility to handle sudden peaks and surges.

If we are looking for the financial equivalent of our three types of generator, the traditional high street banks and stock markets are our West Thurrocks. They provide the essential supply of day-to-day money that is needed for the economy to operate. By charging interest, they set a price for the use of money and thus employ the power of markets to constantly control the balance between spending, saving, consumption, and investment. The interest rate itself is heavily influenced by the central bank, who oversee the money supply as a whole, a bit like National Grid control.

A lot has been said over the last few years about the rise of 'casino capitalism'. This is the area of financial markets where money is never used to invest in actual bricks and mortar, iron and steel, or bits and bytes. Rather, it goes into buying financial products.

To give a simple example, I used to be the manager of a toothpaste tube factory. Our tubes were made of aluminium, and we spent about £3 million a year on raw materials. We would often sign a one-year contract with our customers, which meant that the price we would get for our product was fixed a year into the future. But what if the wholesale price of aluminium went up? If we suddenly found ourselves paying more for raw materials, our slender profit margin could disappear and the factory could go bust. So what we actually did was to go to a metals broker and buy an 'option' that allowed us to purchase our aluminium at a guaranteed price this time next year. What we had essentially created was a bet between the two of us. If the price of aluminium fell or stayed the same then the broker won (they could keep our option payment and we just bought at the current price). But if aluminium became more expensive, the factory won (we could buy aluminium next year at a discount to the new going rate, possibly saving ourselves significantly more than we paid for the option in the first place). The broker set the option price in the expectation that they would win more often than they lost, but because the factory couldn't afford the risk of being caught out by the price of aluminium the deal still made sense to us. We had enough to worry about making tubes, without spending all year watching prices on the London Metals Exchange. The option itself was never anything other than a piece of paper, just a glorified betting slip in the capitalist casino, but it helped secure real jobs and investment and made our business a lot less risky.

Slightly harder to justify are the traders who use these types of deals simply to make money. The bet against the broker would still pay out even if I never planned to buy any actual aluminium at all. If I was good enough at it, I could make a living just buying and selling options on future commodity prices. Like a professional gambler, if I am better at the game then everyone else in the casino, I will win and they will lose. This is a 'zero sum game'; for every winner there is a loser, and nothing of any use or value ever gets created as a result. In fact it acts as net drain on the financial system, because all the various brokers and traders will want to take their profits out along the way.

But even these types of deals do serve at least some kind of useful purpose. Firstly they keep the markets working. For my factory to purchase our metals option, someone had to be willing to sell it to us. The chance of finding a 'normal' business who happened to want to do exactly the same deal in reverse would be pretty remote. In reality, we were probably buying off a speculator. This service of ensuring that there are enough buyers and sellers is called 'liquidity', and unfashionable as it may be to admit it, markets cannot easily function without it.

The second useful service that speculative markets provide is to quantify risk. What will the price of aluminium be this time next year? I don't know, but I can look on the internet and find out how much a one year option is going to cost me. That will tell me if my one year deal with my customers is likely to make a profit, or even worth doing at all. The market may not always get it right, but it offers the best possible guess because markets force out the truth (and I can hold them to it by striking a deal today).

Speculative markets are the 'Dinorwigs' of the financial system. They don't actually make anything real; in fact they absorb it (by turning a percentage of my factory's profits into Porsches and Ferraris for commodity traders). But they do enable the real productive economy to manage the risk of sudden unexpected events and they keep things flowing when the normal money supply would not be fast or flexible enough to provide liquidity. This may not justify their Ferraris, but it does justify their existence.

What is important is to keep the two separate. Someone losing a bet in the capitalist casino is bad for them but good for the person on the other side of the deal (who is of course now up by the same amount). Someone going bankrupt through losing one bet too many is bad for all of us, because the money they have lost has to be paid back and the only way it can reappear is for everyone else to pay a little bit more in interest (or, if governments are forced to intervene, in taxes). This explains a lot of what happened in the 2008 banking collapse. Banks were buying complex financial products which seemed to offer great returns, and they fatally underestimated the risks if the whole market turned down at the same time. The resultant losses damaged their ability to create money (remember how everything depends on having some initial capital to work with, a great chunk of which had now just been lost). This made it more difficult and expensive for normal people and businesses to get hold of the money they needed, hence the term 'credit crunch'.

These two areas of the market serve fundamentally different purposes and have to be kept separate. Speculative markets can carry on managing risk and providing liquidity, just so long as they are not doing it using credit money which has been created to facilitate the running of the 'real' economy. You can't divert the entire output of West Thurrock power station to pumping water up a mountain at Dinorwig; you will end up consuming more electricity than you actually generate and there won't be enough left for people to boil their kettles. At the time of writing, in the aftermath of the financial crash, governments are actively working to change regulations and ensure that retail banking, which serves the real economy, is kept separate from the casino world of investment banking. Right now there is the political will to do so, but the lessons have to be remembered because unless these two parts of the system remain insulated from each other they will inevitably blow each other's circuits once again.

Why pay more?

At the other end of the scale, far from the casinos of the speculative markets, there are huge amounts of money which get paid back gradually, regularly, and almost entirely predictably. Outside of property bubbles driven by cheap credit, most homeowner mortgages are boringly reliable. People pay back the same amount each month, and very few risk default because they know they will lose their home if they do so. Large public projects such as new roads, bridges, or hospitals behave in a similar way. The borrowing is often over a long period, and loans to stable governments produce a modest but reliable return. This is the 'base load' element of the financial power grid, and requires little in the way of active control. Which does rather beg the question, where are the financial equivalents of Oldbury nuclear power station? It seems that, as well as getting the commercial banks mixed up in the 'peak load' world of casino capitalism, we are also using them to provide the 'base load' of stable, long-term finance.

This would be fine if it wasn't for the fact that they still charge interest. We have seen that interest exists for a reason, and that it provides the essential 'grid control' function that keeps the right amount of monetary 'power' flowing around the financial system. But the financial 'base load' doesn't really need any grid control, it just needs to get on and do its job. Because interest is applied to 95% of the money in circulation, it ends up being charged not just on profitable business ventures and consumer credit for luxuries, but on the cost of things that are essential for wellbeing like housing, hospitals, and water supplies.

In the case of private housing, this means that the person who buys a house using a mortgage ends up paying nearly twice as much for their home as someone who is able to buy it using wealth they already own. Even worse, the interest payments go to people who already have wealth to invest, so the rich get richer and the poor get poorer. The 'two nation' problem rears its head, relationships across society are strained, and governments are forced into crude schemes to redistribute wealth to sort out the mess.

The situation with public assets is actually very similar. If they are acquired directly by governments, they must be funded by public borrowing through the bond markets which incurs an interest charge. If the assets are privately funded then the owner will be looking for an equivalent return on their investment, which gets loaded into the charges to use them so the government still pays. When we say 'government', we really mean the taxpayer. Again, this has the effect of transferring wealth over time from the poor to the rich. Both pay taxes towards the cost of government borrowing, but because the already wealthy are likely to own assets such as government bonds, the money may well end up back in their own pockets.

Of course you don't have to use commercial banks to create the money supply. Any government can use its central bank[47] to create as much money as it likes, interest free.[48] Modern money is no longer backed by gold or anything else, and with a *fiat* currency you can either physically print more banknotes or electronically create it in an account, ready to spend.

Until recently, to even suggest this idea was a kind of financial heresy. Everyone 'knew' what the effect would be: the nation would immediately enter a spiral of hyperinflation. The more money the central bank created the less it would be worth, until you needed thousands of banknotes just to buy a loaf of bread. This is exactly what happened in Germany in the 1920s and Zimbabwe in the early 2000s, to quote just two examples. Hyperinflation occurs when a government cynically prints money to spend with no credible plans for ever paying it back. The trust on which the value of the currency is based is destroyed. First people lose their belief that it will function as a store of value; it is clear that the money will be worth a lot less this time next year. They then become reluctant even to use it as means of exchange; if I think that money is about to become worthless then why should I accept it in payment? When it really takes off the rate of collapse can become spectacular. When I was backpacking round Iceland in 1988 the inflation rate was 30% per year. I bought a stamp to send a postcard home, and by the time I came to post it the price of stamps had gone up. This was a minor inconvenience, but imagine living in Zimbabwe in 2008. At one point prices were doubling *every day*, and a $100 trillion banknote was in circulation.

Heresy became orthodoxy in early 2009. As the credit crunch bit harder and the money supply became ever tighter, the traditional approach used by central bank 'grid controllers' – reducing interest rates – had already been used up. The only way to get more money flowing round the economy was to start creating the stuff directly. By the end of 2012 the US Federal Reserve had created around $3 trillion of new money, and the Bank of England was at £375 billion.

This money was quite literally created out of thin air. They simply typed the figures into an account at the central bank and used the money to buy 'safe' assets, mostly their own government bonds. This effectively released capital to the banks, and was supposed to help them rebuild their reserves and encourage them to lend. Opinions differ on how much effect it has actually had, but it has proved one thing beyond doubt. Creating interest-free money directly via the central bank, to the tune of about 15% of gross domestic product, has clearly not produced hyperinflation. In fact some commentators believe that it has had very little economic effect at all.

Everyone currently assumes that as economic conditions stabilise, this 'quantitative easing', as it has been politely named, will gradually be scaled back. But what if it isn't? In principle the issue of interest-free loans by the central bank offers a source of 'base load' money for the types of purposes we have already looked at. It was introduced because the normal monetary control system (raising and lowering interest rates) was already at its limit, but it is now clear that the two can be used together and central banks are increasingly experienced at doing so. The original plan may have been to get rid of the quantitative easing (interest free money) and then start raising interest rates as the economy began to grow, but there is no reason why it cannot be used indefinitely if the right basic rules are followed.

The power of three

We started our journey into the origins of money with the *contractum trinius* or 'triple contract'; the legal trick used by medieval bankers to start the process of lending at interest which has led to modern commercial banks dominating the money supply in modern economies. And it ends with the idea that this near monopoly can be broken by introducing three distinct sectors back into the financial system.

Commercial banks creating interest-bearing credit money still have a vital role to play. They will continue to carry the main burden of regulating the day-to-day money supply, and the cost of that interest is a reasonable price to pay for this complex and vital service.

At the more risky end of the market, the speculative traders of casino capitalism will undoubtedly continue their endless race to beat the system and fleece the other punters. The risk and liquidity services they provide do have some beneficial value, but must be clearly and permanently separated from the sources of credit finance which can turn their activities into a reckless gambling of the entire financial system. Bet if you must, but only with resources which you ultimately own and can afford to lose.

And finally, central banks must move beyond the token supply of notes and coins into a much larger-scale provision of interest-free money to fund the core drivers of wellbeing in society. It is both unjust and unnecessary for these types of basic human needs to be paid for with interest, which means that the poor often end up paying twice. The rules must be clear: all such loans must be paid back over time, they must be used for providing capital assets which contribute directly to essential material wellbeing, and they must be operated as a package with other aspects of monetary policy such as interest-rate setting to ensure that stable economic management can continue.

We are now finally in a position to describe how our new world of housing finance would work in practice. And as we will discover, the same principles apply to the provision of most of the other services that are essential to the material wellbeing of society.

6

ESTABLISH UNIVERSAL OWNERSHIP

A life is sacred. Property is intended to serve life, and no matter how much we surround it with rights and respect, it has no personal being.

MARTIN LUTHER KING JR.

Government has no other end, but the preservation of property.

JOHN LOCKE

By global standards I am a High Net Worth Individual. Between us, my wife and I already own the majority of our house. We have two cars, a pension plan for retirement, and some under-performing investments from the 1990s when we bought our first home. The combined contents of our rooms, pockets, cupboards, and wardrobes would make a disappointingly small amount on eBay but still represent material affluence beyond the dreams of most of our global neighbours. Combined current value of everything: maybe around £½ million.

I hate the term 'net worth'. By suggesting that the worth of an individual can be assessed by adding up the financial value of everything they own, it dehumanises and degrades us while implying that nothing in life matters unless it can be turned into cash. As we have already seen, in wellbeing terms this is a long way from the truth. But whatever I think of the terminology, asset ownership is important. Right now I am in the middle of writing a book which I expect will take at least two months to finish. Some people would see this as a risky endeavour, and it is unlikely that income from writing will ever replace the lost earnings. But it is also an immense privilege. For many people their monthly salary just about covers paying the bills. Without assets to provide financial stability and resilience, they would simply not have the option to take time off to write a book, train for a new career, care for relatives, or make any of the other life choices that I am able to at least consider.

Globally, the inequality in asset ownership is even greater than that for income. Just 1% of the richest people own over 40% of all of our planet's wealth.[49] The top 10% own a massive 85%; I am one of them, and if you are reading this book then there is a good chance that you are too. At the other end of the scale, the poorest 50% of the world's population own just 1% of all global wealth. This great mass of the dispossessed have no real choices at all; they are forced to live hand-to-mouth, committed to a lifetime of hard labour, not to improve their circumstances but simply to survive. This may not be slavery in the traditional sense, but it doesn't look or feel very much different.

Gentlemen of the press

Asset ownership gives people a level of financial resilience and independence. It makes it less likely that they will experience the hardship of absolute material poverty or the relational harm of relative poverty. It means that they are far less likely to enter the downwards spiral of welfare dependency and end up caught in the poverty traps of long-term unemployment and social housing.

Unfortunately, asset poverty is generally self-perpetuating. Because most of the money in circulation is currently created with interest attached, those who have to borrow to acquire assets will end up paying significantly more than those who can obtain them using existing wealth. Given that most of the interest ultimately ends up being paid to existing asset owners as a 'return on investment', this unequal distribution tends to grow steadily over time. Alarmingly, even stable and prosperous societies have a habit of becoming more unequal in asset ownership with each successive generation.

In the previous chapter we saw that this mechanism does not have to operate in the way that it currently does. It is perfectly possible for central banks to create directly a proportion of the money supply as 'base load' money, with no need to charge interest at all.[50] In fact since the 2008 financial crisis they have already been doing so on a massive scale under the title of 'quantitative easing'. So far this QE money has been used almost entirely to recapitalise banks by buying financial assets from them and thus increasing their capital reserves so that they can lend again (with interest, of course). But there is no reason in principle why it could not be used instead to lend directly to individuals and other institutions. This would allow them to acquire assets of their own without the crippling burden of cumulative interest. The money would still have to be paid back, but those on low to average incomes would now be operating on a level financial playing field compared with the already wealthy. Instead of the rich getting richer and the poor getting poorer with no end in sight, the opportunity to acquire assets would now be more equally available to all.

Obviously there are limits on how far we can go with this policy. There will eventually be a maximum percentage of 'base load' money that the economy can swallow without driving up inflation or harming the ability of interest-rate setting to effectively control the financial system (maybe another Nobel prize on offer to the economists who manage to work out where this limit lies). However, the more immediate risk is that politicians seeking election will find what looks like an enormous pot of free money simply irresistible. Why balance the budget by raising taxes or cutting expenditure (either of which risk making you unpopular) when you could just create loads of interest free debt and pretend that the whole problem of living within your means has gone away?

To fit with our emerging model of a society where state, market, and community work together to promote wellbeing, the following criteria must apply to how this interest-free base-load money is used:

1. It must be used to acquire assets, not to fund day-to-day deficit spending.
2. It must be paid back, within the lifetime of the assets it has been used to acquire.
3. The assets must be ones which can be shown to have a direct positive impact on wellbeing.
4. The total amount in circulation must not exceed the threshold at which interest-rate setting can still be used as the main monetary control mechanism.

A wider distribution of asset ownership is very likely to lead to higher levels of wellbeing. Not only can it be facilitated and accommodated by the existing financial system, it will also work to protect that system from further catastrophic events. The complex and risky financial products which triggered the 2008 financial crisis and the asset bubbles which created the conditions for it to happen were both associated primarily with high-wealth financial investors. People with no surplus assets cannot invest anyway. Those with moderate levels of wealth (the 10% who are concentrated in the rich world but not the 1% who own a hugely disproportionate share) tend to have their wealth locked in stable assets like houses and pensions. If the size of this group increases, the amount of wealth available to be gambled in the capitalist casino will be reduced. This reduces the size of the largest possible shock to system, which means that the chances of it falling over again are significantly reduced.

We have seen that creating a more even asset distribution, focused on assets which support wellbeing, is both desirable and possible. We must now consider what this would look like in practice.

An Englishman's home

The main asset which most people aspire to own is their home. In the UK, roughly two-thirds of households own their home either outright or with a mortgage. There is a direct correlation between home ownership and wellbeing; 80% of home owners report medium or high levels of life satisfaction, compared with just 68% of those who live in rented accommodation.[51]

When looking at the worst concentrations of poverty and deprivation in the UK, we saw that these are strongly associated with areas of rented social housing provided or subsidised by the state. Many of the problems experienced disproportionately by residents of big council estates such as poor health, relationship and family breakdown, unemployment, and relative poverty, will directly harm wellbeing. Ending the social housing trap will go some way towards alleviating these issues, but our aspirations should not end there. Home ownership does not just improve subjective wellbeing, it also gives people their own financial safety net, a sense of pride, a stronger and more stable role in their community, and the opportunity to support themselves in retirement and offer a financial head start to the next generation. The issue of inherited wealth is especially significant. As we have already seen, someone who has to borrow the money to buy their home will have to pay nearly twice as much for it over a 25-year period as someone who is able to purchase it outright. The difference amounts to hundreds of pounds per month, which means that the person borrowing via a mortgage will have to either work harder (putting more strain on their health and relationships) or spend less (which at minimum produces inequality and relative poverty, and in some cases leads to debt or actual material poverty too).

We have also seen that the main factor preventing more people from owning their own home is the housing market. After decades in which home ownership in the UK increased steadily, even the cheapest property is now unaffordable for a growing number of people. With average house prices now at six times average income, it seems very unlikely that two-thirds of the current generation will be able to own their homes in the way that their parents did. We have seen too that house prices are determined by market forces of supply and demand. Demand for housing in the UK significantly exceeds supply, and seems likely to do so for the foreseeable future, especially given that our aspiration to live in a bigger house in a better area seems almost unlimited. With this being the case, house prices will rise to the limit of affordability. They have risen especially fast over the last decade because the availability of 'cheap money' (mortgage loans at historically low rates of interest) has pushed up the maximum amount that house buyers could afford to pay. For previous generations, the accepted wisdom was that borrowing should not exceed three times the main wage earner's annual salary. At the height of the recent housing boom with low interest rates starting to look like a permanent feature, loans of five times salary were available to some borrowers, with second incomes also being taken into account. With these historically high multiples on offer, the spending power available to borrowers was greatly increased and it is hardly surprising that house prices rose rapidly as a result. Prices fell back briefly after the financial crash but still remain well above historic levels when compared to household incomes or rental rates. In the meantime, investors continue to buy up property to meet growing rental demand (people have to live somewhere after all), and the transfer of housing assets from poor to rich continues apace.

The obvious way to break the cycle is to make some of the new base-load money available to private individuals to fund the purchase of their own home. This would mean that even those on low to average incomes will be able to acquire a house or flat of their own, rather than much of their housing costs going on either interest payments or rent. The policy would be simple to implement, and basically would allow anyone who does not already own their home to borrow up to the average national house price,[52] interest free. The money would be created by the central bank as described in the last chapter, and administered by normal high street lenders to make it feel as much like a conventional mortgage as possible. The house is not 'free': it still has to be paid for, but crucially it is only the principal sum that needs to be repaid, with no interest being added. The total cost of acquisition could be nearly halved over the lifetime of the loan, vastly increasing the opportunity for home ownership. This would be a once-per-lifetime entitlement; it enables more people to get on the ladder of home ownership at an affordable cost, and thereafter any decisions to buy progressively more expensive properties are down to the individual using the normal commercial mortgage market.

The amount borrowed would be secured on the property and could therefore not exceed the property value.[53] The usual checks on affordability for the individual would continue to apply (although they would be much easier to satisfy). Where a purchaser wanted to buy a house worth more than the national average, they could top up their loan from the conventional mortgage market, although this part would be interest bearing. To avoid assisting the already wealthy, it might be considered desirable to reduce the interest-free component on higher value properties. Thus if the property was worth £100,000 more than national average, the interest free loan available might be reduced by £50,000. This roll off would continue until no support was available for the most expensive houses.

Not only is this idea relatively straightforward to implement, it will also be wildly popular (and therefore politically expedient). In fact there is only one remaining problem to be overcome. If we make these mortgages interest free and allow them to run for a traditional 25-year term, the monthly repayments on the average UK house would fall by nearly half.[54] And as we have already seen, cheap money causes house prices to rise. There is absolutely no point in halving people's mortgage payments if this just means that house prices then double again over the course of a few years. We would be back where we started, with an unsustainable housing boom funded by cheap credit and no net gain for anyone except existing property owners.

The answer to this conundrum is to set the repayment period based on affordability rather than use a standard 25-year duration. If these loans were offered over a 12- or 15-year term rather than the usual 25, the monthly repayments would remain roughly the same and there would be no credit-fuelled boom in house prices. People would become debt-free home owners sooner rather than later, but we are hardly going to complain about this given that it was one of our main objectives in the first place. Because households would climb the housing ladder faster it may increase demand (and hence prices) at the upper end of the housing market. This isn't really a problem, because acquiring a bigger house (or not) makes little difference to wellbeing once the occupants are already past the point of enough. They can choose this option if they wish, but they could equally choose to enjoy more leisure time, retire earlier, or take a career break, because many people will now be mortgage free in their forties. Given that this is the time of life when people report the lowest average wellbeing scores anyway (the bottom of the U-bend), removing the financial pressures of paying a mortgage at exactly this point must surely be a good thing.

The ability to influence monthly payments by changing the loan duration also gives us two other useful options. For the lowest-paid workers, even an interest-free loan over 15 years would not be enough for them to afford their own home in many areas. By extending the repayment term for these groups, we create an alternative to housing subsidies which allows them to escape the social housing trap once and for all. This will not inflate house prices as they will still be making the maximum repayments they can reasonably afford, but it will allow many people who are currently excluded from home ownership to participate.

For the wider economy, it opens up the possibility of directly influencing the housing market by lengthening or shortening the standard repayment duration as market conditions change. The rapidly rising house prices seen over recent decades have been partly caused by economic decisions which overheated the housing market. Stable, affordable long-term house prices are highly desirable from a wellbeing point of view as they reduce the financial stress on households and ensure that a decent standard of housing remains accessible to all. If monetary conditions are loose and house prices start to rise, by shortening the standard repayment term the central bank can directly increase the monthly cost of repayments and dampen the market back down (you could call this 'quantitative tightening'). Likewise if the money supply is tight and prices are becoming depressed (leading to negative equity and clogging up the market) the repayment term could be extended. Given the huge size of the UK mortgage market (with over £1,000 billion in loans outstanding), having a proportion of this under their direct influence is a useful addition to the central banker's armoury. At present their objective is to ensure low, stable inflation and their only weapon is interest-rate setting (with a bit of quantitative easing or forward guidance thrown into the pot in times of crisis). By adding a secondary target of ensuring house-price stability at a certain level and providing the independent rate-setters with the power to adjust repayment rates to ensure it, it becomes possible to moderate the housing market separately from the rest of the economy.

Social capital

Housing is probably the single biggest driver of wellbeing which is economic in nature and largely under the control of the individual and the market. There are, however, a number of other types of asset which are (in the UK at least) normally controlled by the state but are still essential to wellbeing. These include schools, hospitals and healthcare facilities, safety and security infrastructure, and a wide range of community assets such as municipal buildings and public spaces (rural or urban).

At present, the state provides these facilities through capital investment funded by public borrowing. The borrowing takes the form of government bonds, which enable the government to borrow from commercial markets at a fixed rate and repay the loans gradually over time.[55] The basic idea is sound enough: if a hospital is going to have a useful life of 40 years, it does seem unreasonable for one particular generation of taxpayers to fund the whole cost in a single year. However, the bonds come with an annual interest payment attached to them. Given that the purpose of this particular type of borrowing is to support the wellbeing of the population at large, it is by no means clear why there should also be an interest charge paid to the banking system and the already wealthy. We have created a system where taxes paid by the many are used to fund the purchase of assets for the benefit of the many, but also to pay an interest charge to the relatively few wealthy individuals who own the majority of government bonds (remember that just 1% of the global population currently owns over 40% of the wealth).

Having looked in detail at how base-load money can be used to transform home ownership, it is now very simple to see how the same principle can be extended to publicly owned assets. Again, for those particular types of asset which meet our four basic tests, the central bank can create interest free money and lend it directly for the construction or purchase of schools, hospitals, and other public facilities. The debt would still need to be repaid and would behave very similarly to a 'normal' public works loan, but the repayments would only need to cover the actual sum borrowed with no interest charges being added.

Given the tendency of successive governments to borrow money rather than balance the budget through unpopular tax rises or spending cuts, rules in the public sector would need to be rigorously applied. An asset investment must be clearly defined as a piece of physical infrastructure which has a multi-year lifespan and can appropriately be repaid over the duration of its working life. The loan must be directly tied to the asset, not thrown into a pot of 'general public borrowing'. The term 'investment' is frequently abused in political language. Building a new school, hospital, or public library is a genuine investment, which can appropriately be funded through a long-term interest free loan. Employing more teachers, doctors, or librarians to staff it is not an 'investment'; it is a running cost and has to be funded from in-year taxation or the public finances simply will not balance. If the public sector wants to run a budget deficit then it should be obliged to borrow the money at commercial rates of interest just as any other organisation would.[56] This ensures that the economic 'grid control' system, which continues to depend on interest-rate setting for its main control mechanism, can carry on operating properly without being short-circuited by unmanaged public borrowing.

This radical re-think of how public assets are financed should also provide a welcome opportunity to reconsider how these services are delivered. The basic founding principle of the British welfare state was 'free universal provision at the point of need', and this has become deeply ingrained into our national concepts of fairness. It seems clear that only the state is properly equipped to ensure that essential services are freely available to all who need them. By comparison with Britain's NHS, the American system of private responsibility for healthcare simultaneously manages to be more expensive per person and to provide adequate services to a far smaller percentage of the population. Without a clear sense of collective responsibility it can be very difficult to get everyone to contribute and services for the most vulnerable tend to collapse, just like the roads on our nearby private estate.

However, while the state is generally good at facilitating collective financial responsibility, it is much less well equipped for managing complexity, responding to relational human needs, and driving efficiency and innovation. These are tasks which the market and the community normally do rather better. 'Free at the point of need' is an essential principle for services that are essential to wellbeing, but it is not the same thing as 'can only be delivered by a state bureaucracy'. Britain's National Health Service already has a budget larger than the entire economy of Hungary, Pakistan, or New Zealand. To suggest that an organisation the size of a medium-sized country can be effectively run by top-down centralised control is at best an ideological position rather than one supported by evidence.

A universal healthcare system requires clear and fair rules for how people can access the services and a sustainable mechanism for collective funding. No-one wants to contemplate a system where treatment is handed out based on patronage or is dependent on ability to pay. These are requirements which only the state as an actor can deliver. At the same time the system has to handle the incredible complexity of treating millions of patients each year, discern the truth about healthcare priorities in a world where everyone both inside and outside the system is arguing their own agenda, and turn scientific and technological innovation into practical benefits for patients. This is the kind of stuff that markets excel at, and excluding them will leave us with a system that is clumsier and costlier than it needs to be or could be. Finally, the clinical side of the system will be overwhelmed unless we create communities where physical and mental health can flourish, and care for the young, the elderly, and the chronically ill is seen as a collective responsibility rather than 'somebody else's problem'.

Public health, mental health and social care have traditionally been the 'cinderella services' in terms of priority and funding. The former head of NHS England admitted that given a choice between heart attack prevention and building a new acute cardiac treatment ward, the big shiny clinical project will always be the one that gets funded under the current system. This is despite the fact that prevention is both better for the patient's wellbeing and cheaper to deliver than cure. When Lord O'Donnell made his proposals for wellbeing-led decision making in public services,[57] he identified mental health as the single biggest opportunity for a step change improvement in our national wellbeing. Funding obviously matters, but wellbeing must be allowed to guide how the money is spent as well as how it is provided.

Common property

The third area where base-load money could be legitimately used to acquire assets for wellbeing is in the area of charity and community groups. Britain has a deep reserve of community assets, starting with church institutions going back hundreds of years and added to by philanthropic endeavours in the nineteenth and early twentieth centuries. This community asset base is now being steadily eroded. It has been crowded out both by the state (which for a while during the twentieth century saw everything to do with community provision as its exclusive responsibility) and by the market (which has increasingly commercialised community activity and stripped out community assets for short-term profit). Voluntary, community, and faith groups now find themselves in the position of the poor relations; needing good-quality assets to perform their role but unable to match the spending power of the state and market, and forced to borrow at interest to fund any kind of long-term investment. Again, the moral case for why organisations, whose objectives are almost entirely focused on community wellbeing, should have to pay interest to the already wealthy in order to access funds to carry on their work is simply impossible to make.

Making base-load money available to voluntary, community, and faith groups is a simple and very efficient way of promoting broader community asset ownership. The public benefit requirement applied to all UK registered charities means we can be confident that any charitable organisation is already engaged in activities to promote wellbeing in the broadest sense. The rules regarding what an 'asset' is and how long it should take to pay for can be lifted straight from the capital accounting guidelines already followed by charities.

Every year charity groups put together plans to develop youth centres and health centres, minibus services and web services, worship halls and sports halls, studios and skateparks. By up to halving the cost of monthly payments on long-term asset loans, many more of these schemes would be able to go ahead. As well as offering services to support wellbeing directly, they also create the additional benefit of increased social capital through broader and deeper relational networks in local communities. This should be one of the early priorities for the use of 'base load' money, and given that the community sector is currently smaller than either the public sector or the housing market it also provides a great opportunity to test and prove the system on a manageable scale.

Most people find it pretty easy to get behind the idea of youth clubs and medical research. But there are other areas of charitable and community work which are proving increasingly contentious. When Stephen Metcalfe MP was first elected to represent East Thurrock in 2010, he proudly stood on a platform of ensuring that Britain gave 0.7% of our national income to overseas aid and development. By 2015 he was still a firm personal supporter of the policy, but the reaction on the doors had changed noticeably. Instead of a generally positive response, you were now equally likely to get an ear-bashing that usually began with 'charity begins at home', followed by an example of how some particular service in the UK wasn't being funded and it was therefore a national scandal that we should be spending money to help the poorest of the poor in other nations.

The mis-used proverb is particularly revealing of the changing national mood (and maybe evidence of the corrosive effect of collective unhappiness in Thurrock and in Britain as a whole). 'Charity begins at home' originally meant 'you learn to love your neighbour through the positive example of your friends and family'. Today it is increasingly used in the sense of 'look after your own before you help anyone else'. This represents a profound shift in thinking, and once these attitudes become normalised when discussing international aid and refugees, they can rapidly be used to justify a lack of concern for anyone other than yourself.

How is it that initiatives which are genuinely about helping and supporting people have become sufficiently contentious that some would question whether they are worth supporting at all? If we are not even able to achieve a broad consensus about the type of community we are hoping to build, then the whole ability of the community to serve as an effective actor is brought into question. Before we consider in any more detail how the power of communities can be released, we need to take a long hard look at what kind of community twenty-first-century Britain has actually become.

7

START A CULTURAL REVOLUTION

The mouth speaks what the heart is full of.

JESUS

I believe that political correctness can be a form of linguistic fascism, and it sends shivers down the spine of my generation who went to war against fascism.

P. D. JAMES

'It's time to take our country back!' That's what the posters on billboards across Thurrock were telling people in the weeks running up to the EU referendum vote. Take it back from whom? The posters didn't say. According to the reassuring voices of mainstream national politicians, it meant taking back our 'sovereignty' – the elements of economic and political control which had been lost to the EU under successive treaties. But as we have already seen, for potential Brexit voters in Thurrock the issue of the EU as a political entity only ranked about number six on their list of priorities. Top of the list by a mile was immigration, and most of the other issues which they felt were important were associated with immigration too. They worried about housing (being filled with immigrants), jobs (being taken by immigrants), public services (being flooded with immigrants), and the welfare state (being bled dry by immigrants). They knew exactly who they wanted to take their country back from, and it wasn't the President of the European Council.

A thorough analysis of any of these problems will tell you that simply reducing immigration is very unlikely to deliver the hoped-for solutions. It's easy to conclude that people were facing complex issues of social change and globalisation and looking for someone to blame. But this view misses perhaps the most powerful and important driver of wellbeing of all: a network of strong and positive relationships at community level. As one woman put it to me when I knocked on her door during the 2015 general election campaign: 'I've lived in Barking[58] all of my life. But I had to move out. It just doesn't feel like this country any more. I'm sure you know what I mean by that.'

What actually makes a place 'feel like this country'? The Britain which that voter and many like her identify with is proud, open, hospitable, generous, and confident. Take away that sense of identity and you take away the very characteristics which have traditionally enabled us to prosper through international trade and define our place in the world. Her deeply held conviction that immigration is now the key problem doesn't come from an over-zealous nationalism; it reflects a crisis of confidence in who we are as a nation.

Rule Britannia

I am British (and English). I enjoy hot tea with milk, warm beer, and fish and chips on the sea front. I am excessively polite in queues but can probably come across as rude in my unwillingness to speak to strangers because we haven't been properly introduced yet. I talk constantly about the weather, complain about trivia when life is going well, but will resolutely 'keep calm and carry on' when circumstances get tough. I feel a surge of pride when I hear our national anthem and I share in the masochistic agony of supporting our national football team.

National quirks and stereotypes aside, what is it that gives us such a strong sense of national identity? My Englishness is not something that has come down through long generations; my ancestors are mostly of Scottish or Irish descent who came seeking a new life in Liverpool when it was a global port and the second richest city on earth. I hold a British passport, but so do many thousands of others who would not see themselves as culturally British. Even native speakers struggle to place my accent, with its mix of north and south from an itinerant childhood overlaid with the 'estuary English' of my adopted Essex home.

In his first-century vision, Saint John described a great crowd 'from every nation, tribe, people, and language', standing before the throne of heaven.[59] As well as showing that the idea of racial and cultural diversity has been around for at least 2,000 years, these four categories of nation, tribe, people-group, and language remain as insightful building blocks for understanding how our national identity is put together.

Nationhood is the symbols, values, and traditions of the geographical nation that I call home. In the modern world it is normally identified with a political nation-state. All the things we would associate with 'patriotism' – flags, anthems, national celebrations, military pomp, and sporting pride – form part of this concept. Equally important are our traditions of law and government; Britishness is as much about equality under law and parliamentary democracy as it is about the Union Jack and 'God save the Queen'.

Tribe is the ties that bind. Relationships to family and community can define us just as profoundly as the larger and sometimes more abstract concept of nation. In some places tribal identity is literally that; to be a Zulu in South Africa is to hold a tribal identity with personal, cultural, linguistic and political dimensions. In the UK our tribal identities are often multiple and overlapping. Regional accents and identities are important, and we have religious communities, communities of interest and affiliation, and a range of others woven into the mix too.

People-group refers primarily to ethnic origin. Basic ethnicity manifests itself in our skin colour and other physical features. Below that we are surprisingly sensitive to more nuanced genetic and ethnic traits. Most white Europeans would consider that there is a distinctive French, German, Scandinavian, or Italian 'look'.

One British survey showed that English people are able to guess the regional origins of people with roots in areas such as East Anglia from just a photograph, with a significantly greater accuracy than random chance. Scientific analysis seems to confirm that they are right; different genetic markers are clustered by region within nations and continents.[60]

Language is our native tongue. Because community is defined by relationships and relationships require communication, shared language is a key component of identity. Regional variation can be a feature of linguistic identity. Norwegians have two grammatically different official dialects of their language. A Geordie from Newcastle speaks very differently from an Essex boy or girl, but both would be clear that they are English and that an American or Australian speaker of the language is not.

By playing around with these four components of national identity, you can start to understand how different nations see themselves. When British athlete Mohammed 'Mo' Farah won the 5,000 and 10,000 metre gold medals at the London 2012 Olympic games, the whole nation went wild in celebration. Twenty-nine year old Farah is not native born; he came to England from Somalia at the age of eight. So is he British, or not? Admittedly everyone likes to claim a winner as one of their own. But in his post-race interview, Farah spoke to the nation in perfect native English with a distinct London accent. That matters; the whole world speaks English as a second language, so the Brits are especially sensitive to what native UK English sounds like. He is a British citizen and speaks of his pride at representing his country. That matters too; first generation immigrants are often conflicted on the subject of which nation they call 'home'. Farah's victory celebration, the 'Mo-bot' gesture, is distinctively British too. The Brits love Jamaican sprint champion Usain Bolt, but his 'lightning bolt' trademark would probably be considered too cocky for a British athlete to get away with. The 'Mo-bot', with its dash of self-deprecating humour and its nod to goal celebrations in the English Premier league (Farah is a keen Arsenal fan), gets it spot on. I would suggest that Britain ranks its markers of identity in the order language-nation-tribe-people.

With the first three so clearly visible, few would suggest that Mo Farah's black African Muslim origins seriously detract from his Britishness.

Not every nation thinks the same way as us Brits, and one of the sources of misunderstanding is when we assume that they do. For my Albanian friends, the fact that you are of ethnic Albanian descent is everything. Family and community relationships are vital too, and shape the culture both positively (in generous hospitality and a sense of mutual obligation) and negatively (through patronage and violent feuds). The Albanian language is important, and if you have all of those things, whether you happen to be a citizen of Albania itself, Kosovo, Macedonia, or the Albanian diaspora is less relevant. My personal observation is that Albanians rank their identity as people-tribe-language-nation (almost the reverse of the Brits).

America is historically an immigrant nation, and the fact that you choose to become American and 'pledge allegiance to the flag' is seen as definitive. Adopting a tribal identity, such as affiliating to a town or state or football team helps to affirm that decision. Language is of practical importance (and a sign of integration), while your people-group shows where you came from but not where you are headed.[61] I would suggest that the USA is a nation-tribe-language-people kind of place. Where this leaves Albanian-Americans is a fascinating question. Their national American identity and their ethnic Albanian identity will not really conflict for either group, because they rank them at opposite ends of their respective identity scales. The divide will probably come based on whose set of cultural or 'tribal' norms they adopt, which matters to both groups.

My culture right or wrong

What we even mean by a nation's 'culture' is not always clear. 'Cultural activities' is often used as an umbrella term for arts, music, language, and literature. We identify a nation's culture in its food, its dress, and its customs, which are markers of 'tribal' identity. We talk of political culture, meaning a nations laws and how it governs itself. And the phrase 'multi-cultural' is often actually used to describe a mix of different races and ethnicities.

In truth, our culture is made up of all of these things. My Englishness is shaped by Shakespeare and 'Eastenders',[62] by Queen and country, by fish and chips and Sheffield United football club, and by Celtic, Roman, Saxon, Viking, Norman, and Asian settlers. I don't personally own or claim every aspect of English cultural identity, but crucially I do understand what our shared pool of British culture looks like, and own a big enough subset of it for myself and others to know that I belong.

Given that the building blocks of our culture and our national identity are basically the same thing, it is questionable whether such a thing as a 'multi-cultural society' can ever actually exist in practice. A truly multi-cultural society would not be one society at all, it would be two or more societies occupying the same piece of territory. The record of this type of society is not an encouraging one:

1. Rwanda, 1994. Tutsi and Hutu. 800,000 killed in mass genocide.
2. Bosnia, 1992–1995. Serbs, Croats, and Bosniaks. 100,000 dead in civil war and massacres.
3. Northern Ireland, 1960s–1998. Nationalist and Loyalist communities. 3,500 killed in 'the troubles'.
4. South Africa, 1948–1994. White apartheid rule over black majority. Minimum 7,000 killed.
5. Israel, 1948–current. Israelis and Palestinians. Around 15,000 direct casualties.

Clearly this is not what the proponents of multiculturalism are aspiring towards. When we use the term 'multi-cultural society', what we probably really mean is a 'multi-ethnic culture'. A society which has a sufficient pool of shared cultural values and markers to allow members from different ethnic and racial backgrounds to identify themselves as members of it, and hence to identify with one another.

Everything we have looked at so far arises naturally from the complex web of relationships formed by the community itself. The state cannot pass a law defining or changing national identity, and the market cannot buy or sell it at a price. However, how these aspects of identity are expressed in practice is something which governments can and do get involved with. Politicians cannot legislate for the kind of strong, open, resilient community relationships that lead to relational wellbeing. But they can create an environment for the community to build and grow them, both by the kind of leadership they offer and the policies they follow.

Approaches to community relations in the UK over the last decade or so have emphasised five main themes: multiculturalism, diversity, tolerance, equality, and political correctness. All are struggling to deliver their stated aims, and we need to look at each of them to understand why and what can be done about it.

Culture club

As we have seen, multiculturalism in the sense of encouraging different groups in society to retain and strengthen their own distinctive cultures is a highly questionable objective. Indiscriminate multiculturalism is just as likely to encourage cultural values which divide society as it is to promote unity. We have already seen that British national identity includes elements of language, nation, tribe, and people-group, probably in that order. A cultural agenda which supports people to identify with and adopt the elements that are most important to shared national identity is likely to promote strong, positive community relationships because they will also identify with each other. Multiculturalism claims to support this aim, but in practice it often works against rather than towards it.

Multicultural programmes normally encourage people to learn their parent's native language and support them in doing so, for example by funding 'community language' classes and providing multiple translations of official documents. But if shared language is an important part of British identity, then to promote integration we should be doing the exact opposite. We should be funding English language classes to help immigrant people learn English and their children to become proficient as 'native English speakers'. Official translation services should be handholding people through understanding the English document, not providing an alternative which means that they never have to. This is not to say that people shouldn't continue to be multi-lingual. This can be especially helpful in promoting inter-generational relationships and wellbeing, but not at the expense of mastering English.

Multiculturalism encourages people to preserve every aspect of their ancestors' national culture. Sometimes this can be helpful. Many people find that experiencing the music, food, and festivals of other cultures is an enjoyable part of getting to know their neighbours. But other aspects of culture are simply incompatible, and in the end you have to make a choice. Britain has been on a long cultural journey to a point where equality of all people under law is an intrinsic part of our social values. If your own culture expects you to live by a 'caste' system or gives women an intentionally subordinate role, it is impossible to live by both sets of values at the same time. If I ever emigrated to another country, it would presumably be because the lifestyle and values appealed to me and I intended to adopt them. We should give people who choose to come to our own country the same credit. It is actually insulting and a profound form of rejection to tell someone who has chosen to live their life in Britain that they cannot really become part of us, and must instead continue to live as cultural exiles.

A multi-cultural society is in many ways a futile and self-defeating objective. Almost always what people are actually aspiring towards is a multi-ethnic culture; one where people from different ethnic backgrounds identify with one another because they share a common sense of national identity. Government policy should understand and actively promote those shared values, not encourage people to live by conflicting cultural norms inherited from their past.

Same difference

Each year, organisations up and down the country run initiatives and events aimed at 'promoting diversity'. I suspect what is actually meant by this is encouraging people from different backgrounds to get along with each other. It might be a good idea if we just came out and said that, because diversity in and of itself is a rather odd thing to promote.

In most respects, promoting diversity at community level is an impossibility. The diversity is already there. Diversity is not an aim or an objective, it is a statistic. I can go out and measure the diversity of my local area tomorrow,[63] but I cannot change it.[64]

Diversity is neither a good thing nor a bad thing, it is just a thing. More diverse groups and communities enjoy certain advantages, especially in the area of creativity and innovation. Research carried out in commercial organisations has shown that diverse teams consistently come up with more novel and numerous ideas for solving problems. They also have disadvantages. More diverse groups find it harder to make decisions and reach agreement, and ethnically diverse communities can be vulnerable to racial tension and conflict.

These negative effects do not even require actual diversity; they can arise equally through fear or perception of diversity. This fact has been exploited by populists and despots for years. If one section of society believes that another is rapidly growing in size and influence, they will tend to feel threatened. Promoting diversity for its own sake can have exactly this effect. By causing people to feel that 'those others' are more numerous or more assertive than is actually the case, it is likely to make community relations worse rather than better. If what we are really trying to promote is increasing social capital through broader and deeper relationships across cultural boundaries, then all these diversity initiatives may actually be self-defeating.

The line between diversity and division is a fine one, and it comes down to whether we see ourselves as 'fundamentally the same (with differences)' or 'fundamentally different (with similarities)'. Diversity can be cause for celebration, but only when it happens in the context of an over-arching narrative of unity and shared identity.

Tolerable to meet you

Like diversity, tolerance is presented as a good thing. We have all seen the effects of intolerance; it produces fear, harassment, prejudice, discrimination, violence, and in extreme cases has led to mass murder. Given that intolerance is so clearly harmful and destructive, surely tolerance is a worthwhile goal?

The first problem is that tolerance is pretty insipid as a value. I have never yet been to dinner with someone only to be told at the end of the evening 'it was tolerable to meet you'. Nor have I ever said in return 'thanks for the meal, I really tolerated it'. When we tolerate something, it means that we dislike it and would rather it was not there, but we refrain from actively doing anything about it. This can be helpful up to a point; self-restraint has to be preferable to lashing out against anything that we dislike or disagree with. But tolerance alone hardly provides a compelling value system on which to base our social relationships.

The second problem is that tolerance as a virtue is logically self-defeating. If I consider tolerance to be an intrinsically good thing, then I will tolerate everyone regardless of their opinions and beliefs. I will tolerate people of other races, cultures, and religions. I will also tolerate racists, bigots, and extremists. In doing so I risk allowing them space and opportunity to destroy the very tolerant society I am trying to build. This is unacceptable to my ethic of toleration, so I will adopt a policy of 'zero tolerance towards intolerance'. Having started with tolerance as a universal value, I rapidly end up with two lists; one of things that I am willing to tolerate and the other of things that I am not. And of course that puts me in exactly the same position as the racists, bigots, and extremists. We both have our lists of what we tolerate and what we don't, it is just that our lists are different.

At its most extreme, tolerance begins to look like a distinctly dubious value system all of its own. It starts as a willingness to endure ideas and views I disagree with out of a commitment to freedom of conscience and expression. But this can drift into a near-ideological dogma that all ideas and opinions are of equal value regardless of their merit, and that any disagreement or criticism of the views of others should be actively suppressed.

What we have tried to do is to use tolerance as a substitute for morality. Moral values can be contentious, and imposing them means restricting someone's freedom. In our individualistic society this goes against the credo of 'be yourself, follow your own path'. We bring up our children to be whoever they want to be, and to tolerate others who do the same. This works fine, right up until the point they decide that what they want to be is wilfully prejudiced, a violent ideologue, or an amoral sexual predator. Having told them their whole life that it is their own free choice which matters and that tolerating people's choices is the 'right' thing to do, we are now robbed of the moral authority needed to confront their behaviour.

Indiscriminate tolerance is like indiscriminate bombing; it causes casualties. The problem with fighting intolerance is that you can find yourself morally aligned with something equally destructive. Far better to fight the negative effects of intolerance. Fight the hatred, fight the violence, fight the discrimination, fight the fear. This way communities will be able to defeat intolerance without raising up a monster of indiscriminate tolerance in its place.

Equal wrongs

When it comes to equality, we are at least on slightly firmer moral ground. The British tradition of equal treatment under a common law dates back to Magna Carta. The spiritual idea that all people are created of equal value in the image of God has been an influential part of our Christian heritage for centuries. Equality is embedded in our laws, our democracy, and our cultural traditions, and to some extent we would all claim to believe in it.

The problem has been that equality in theory does not always translate into equality in practice. We all expect to enjoy equal rights. It is not so clear that everyone has equal opportunities in life. And it is very clear indeed that we do not all end up with equal outcomes. If life was a motor race, some people would say that equality means that everyone starts at the same time, follows the same rules, and has to cover the same number of laps (that's equal rights, or Formula One). Others would say that in a really equal race everyone should be driving the same type of car (that's equal opportunities, or touring car racing). And still others would say that no race is truly equal unless everyone crosses the finish line together (that's equal outcomes, or a bus ride).

There has never been universal agreement on which of these ideals we should be aiming for, let alone how to achieve them in practice. Many people would consider a society where a small elite live in luxury at the expense of an oppressed majority to be morally repugnant. At the other end of the scale, the only successful attempts to achieve genuine equality of outcomes have been in small, simple, tightly knit communities with collective ownership and a strong emphasis on mutual relationships. All attempts to replicate this at a national scale or industrial levels of development have been a disaster. Twentieth-century communism preached equality for all in theory but generated mass inequality, poverty, and oppression in practice.

The most recent trend in Britain (and much of Europe) has been to pass equalities laws aimed at directly protecting minorities or disadvantaged groups. The aim is usually sensible; social problems are identified and laws framed to give additional protection to those most at risk of becoming a victim. The difficulty is that in pursuit of the third objective (equal outcomes), the first objective (equal rights) is over-ridden. Britain's 2010 Equality Act gives specific additional legal rights to anyone with 'protected characteristics' such as race, religion, disability, gender, or sexual orientation.

The weaknesses in this approach are obvious. Although well-intentioned, it means that for the first time under British law 'some are more equal than others'. If you can demonstrate that a random attack in the street was motivated by your 'protected characteristic', it is now treated as a more serious crime than if it was not. Whatever your views on the merits of this idea, try explaining it to a victim of the same crime who does not benefit from the same additional protections. It produces a bizarre reverse manifestation of the 'two nation' problem, where a particular group can both experience genuine disadvantage yet also be perceived as an unfairly privileged minority. An alarming 22% of British people believe that they will 'be treated worse than people of other races' by public sector organisations.[65] This number is far too big to be explained by the negative experiences of minority groups alone, and reflects a wider loss of confidence in the impartiality of public institutions. Put bluntly, people believe that the government engages in 'positive discrimination' and they are made worse off as a result. If this trend continues, the result will be a downward spiral of distrust, resentment, further victimisation, and an increasingly skewed legal response.

To find a more sustainable answer, we need a system which both protects victims and ensures that the law remains completely unbiased to all. The answer again is that we must focus on the manifestations of inequality. Victimisation will almost always take the form of bullying, harassment, discrimination (unequal treatment in the workplace or elsewhere), or incitement of others to do the same. The law should focus on dealing with these actual manifestations. Persistent unwelcome attention, malicious treatment, physical attacks, or being denied the opportunities others enjoy should be unacceptable regardless of who they are perpetrated against. Many of these legal safeguards already exist; and where they do not the law can be changed or strengthened. Once this is done, the discriminatory idea of protected characteristics should be removed from equalities law altogether. If we offer protection at all it must be protection for all.

Equality of opportunity will then mean ensuring that the (now universal) rights provided under law are also available in practice. It is no use asserting that someone has a 'right' to be protected from bullying if bullying remains rampant and there is no action taken against it. If harassment and violent assaults are known to be a problem in a particular community, that is a reason for a proactive and well-resourced response, not for shrugging our shoulders and writing it off as a 'troubled area'. And given that workplace discrimination can be subtle and insidious, it is important that effective protection be available to those who suffer from it. One of the biggest factors promoting bullying, harassment, and discrimination is a culture of impunity, where it is perceived that a blind eye will be turned and perpetrators will 'get away with it'. We cannot claim to have equality in practice until this sense of impunity is ended.

Equality of outcomes is not something which can be forced to happen, and in some cases it is also unclear what it really means anyway. It seems self-evident that in a fair society (at least by the contemporary British understanding of fairness), an identically qualified man and woman should stand an equal chance of getting the same job. It is not so clear that society would automatically be a better place if quotas were imposed to ensure that 50% of midwives were male and 50% of scaffolding erectors were female.

The same principle of complete equality must also apply in the criminal sphere. Hate crime is real, vicious, and casts a shadow of fear over both the direct victims and the wider community. It can also be difficult to identify, as hinted at by the current definition of 'any criminal offence which is perceived, by the victim or any other person, to be motivated by a hostility or prejudice'.[66] It is important that this reliance on victim perception does not lead to different sentencing. Punishments for crime should be meted out objectively based on circumstances, and not influenced by the victim's opinion of the perpetrator's motives. At present it is possible for either the victim or the perpetrator to modify the punishment through their ability to convince the jury of motives which can never be truly objective. Where hate crimes deserve a harsher sentence it is because they are premeditated, one sided, casually violent, and unprovoked; characteristics which often define them but could be fairly and objectively applied to any crime.

Politically incorrect

There is an old proverb which says 'sticks and stones will break my bones, but words will never hurt me'. Like many old proverbs, it is rubbish. Minor physical wounds are painful at the time, but soon heal. The wounds inflicted by verbal abuse can be deep and enduring. They can stay with the victim for years, and they also affect the abuser. What we say with our mouths can reveal what is going on in our heads and hearts, but equally our beliefs and attitudes are continuously shaped by what we choose to confess publicly about them.

It is this insight that words can and do shape attitudes which forms the basis of political correctness as a social tool. It is hardly a new idea. Roman Emperors demanded a verbal confession of allegiance from their subjects, and medieval inquisitors would force those they considered heretics to recant their ideas either as an addition or an alternative to more brutal forms of 'correction'. In the modern world, the regimes which place the strictest controls on free expression tend to be the most authoritarian ones, such as communist or fascist dictatorships. Even today under Chinese communism, Burmese military rule, Saudi theocracy, or even Thai constitutional monarchy,[67] saying the wrong thing in public can land you in prison or worse.

Given the commitment of liberal democracies to freedom of speech as a core value, you would have thought that they would be the last places to resort to these types of authoritarian control. But this is where the tolerance paradox rears its head again. To be genuinely committed to freedom of speech means that you must also accept public expression of ideas which go against the values on which that freedom is founded. It means freedom of speech for Nazis and Stalinists, who would deny those same rights to others. There are vocal demands that such voices should be silenced, and politicians respond by banning certain forms of expression, initially by convention and eventually by law.

The closest that Britain has recently come to passing authoritarian legislation designed to restrict freedom of speech was in the Racial and Religious Hatred Act of 2006. The government originally intended to criminalise 'abusive and insulting' language in the context of religious belief. This led to opposition from a broad coalition of libertarians, writers, entertainers, and (paradoxically) religious groups, all of whom felt that their freedom to criticise religious ideas or practices would be unreasonably restricted. The bill was eventually amended to remove the references to insult and abuse, and now only covers threatening words or behaviour with a deliberate intent to stir up religious hatred. The bill became famous partly as a rallying cry for freedom of expression in the UK, and partly because the government was defeated by a single vote after the then Prime Minister Tony Blair underestimated opposition to his proposals and did not attend to vote in person.

Although direct legal restrictions on free speech have been narrowly rejected in the UK, a general culture of political correctness has become pervasive in politics, the media, and public authorities. Entire sections of language relating to race, disability, gender, sexuality, and religion have become effectively taboo. Anyone questioning the accepted norms runs the risk of losing their reputation or their livelihood. This is despite the fact that those norms are never explicitly stated and the moral or ideological basis on which they are determined remains undisclosed and not subject to scrutiny. A large and profitable industry has sprung up to train or (more menacingly) 're-educate' people in exactly what forms of language they are permitted to use.

Unfortunately some of the significant beneficiaries of this approach have been violent extremists. As their representatives have been pushed out of public view their ideas are no longer subject to debate and scrutiny. At the same time they have gained the glamour and kudos of being able to portray themselves as 'anti-establishment'. One such group we have direct personal experience of in Thurrock is the British National Party (BNP), an extreme nationalist group whose policies included deportation of non-whites from the UK. In 2004 the BNP started to put up candidates in local elections in Thurrock. They took 2% of the popular vote. In 2006 after the controversy surrounding the racial and religious hatred act, their support surged to 12%. The mainstream parties and media responded by branding them as racists and refusing to debate with them or give them a platform. Public servants found themselves being fired from their jobs for being members of the organisation, even though it remained a legal political party. This further increased their anti-establishment appeal. In 2007 their vote doubled again to 25%, easily the third largest party in Thurrock and within spitting distance of both Labour and Conservatives. In 2008 they finally made the breakthrough and gained their first democratically elected council seat in Thurrock.

In 2009 the leader of the BNP, Nick Griffin, was invited to appear on the BBC's flagship *Question Time* political panel show. The decision caused great controversy at the time, with politicians and commentators being divided over whether this legitimised the party or exposed it to much needed public scrutiny. The show pulled in 8 million viewers, doubling its previous record. It was generally accepted that Griffin avoided making any major gaffes but his views were seen in full for the first time by a wide audience. The electoral response was swift. In the 2010 national and local elections a few months later, the BNP were virtually wiped out. They failed to make their predicted national gains, and locally in Thurrock their vote share collapsed back to 13%. Two years later they had almost disappeared from the local scene, split now into two factions and still barely able to muster 2% between them. Where political correctness and censorship had failed, open public debate and scrutiny had dramatically succeeded.

Dictatorships eventually learn that suppressing dissent works for a time but never succeeds for ever. Democracies need to learn the same lesson with regard to intolerance. If people are committed to living together as neighbours, then hatred will ultimately be defeated. If they are not, no amount of politically correct coercion can cover up the problems indefinitely.

Best supporting actor

In the search for positive community relationships, multi-culturalism, diversity, tolerance, equality, and political correctness have all proved flawed and inadequate in what they can achieve. This is partly due to their inherent internal contradictions, and partly because we are expecting too much of politicians, public servants, and the apparatus of state in general. The community itself has to be the leading actor in this area, because the state can play only a limited role and the market will blindly deliver whatever is demanded of it, from equality and diversity consultants to balaclavas and baseball bats.

The roots of community-led answers are there beneath the surface, but have been squeezed out by a mixture of fear, disempowerment, and top-down imposition. We need to release a new set of old values, bringing concepts like unity, reciprocity, responsibility, and hospitality back to centre of the debate.

United we stand

As we have seen, national identity and culture are close to being the same thing. If a people share sufficient components of linguistic, national, tribal, and ethnic identity they will identify with their nation and with one another. This sense of cohesion is something that has to be actively promoted, because anything which works against it divides the nation against itself.

The state has a role to play by letting go of multiculturalism and actively promoting a shared cultural identity. Many of the steps to be taken are quite practical. Require and support English as a shared common language rather than providing excuses for people to avoid learning or using it. Guard equal treatment under law as a foundation of our society, rather than allowing 'equalities' legislation which offers different treatment to designated minorities to creep in. Promote cultural events which celebrate shared aspects of identity above those which separate people into factions.

The Costa test

If communities of cohesion define who we see as 'us', then reciprocity should guide our relationships with those who sit outside of that boundary. One of the most common complaints you hear as a politician knocking on doors in parts of Thurrock is that immigrants are coming in and taking 'our' jobs, 'our' houses, and so on. Those who make these complaints are clearly of the view that this is unfair, and that outsiders are being given preferential treatment compared to the existing local community. Underlying this must be some kind of assumption of what fairness looks like in practice.

Jesus taught his followers to treat others as you would want them to treat you.[68] This formulation, sometimes known as the 'golden rule', exists in both positive and negative forms in other spiritual and philosophical traditions too. It represents a fundamental understanding of fairness as reciprocity, and in its positive form it encourages its adoption as an aspirational standard.[69]

An ethic of reciprocity can be a powerful guide for relationships both within and between communities. If wellbeing is defined by positive relationships, then reciprocity is one of the essential drivers for community-generated wellbeing. Within a community it both embodies and goes beyond the idea of 'equality'. Equality sets minimum standards; reciprocity constantly re-calibrates and refines those standards based on how I myself would want to be treated in any given situation.

This concept is powerful when it comes to forming our response to international migration. It is much easier to see how we should treat people from other nations who want to live and work in the UK if we genuinely put ourselves in their shoes and imagine what we would expect if the situation was reversed.

British people have a long tradition of internationalism, and many choose to live and work beyond their own shores. Some have used the freedom of movement and employment established by European treaties to make a life in other European countries. Before the EU referendum, around a quarter of a million Brits were permanently resident in Spain, with up to a million living there for at least part of the year (presumably to escape the worst of the British weather).[70] Others take their skills further afield. The number of British workers in the United Arab Emirates doubled after the start of the 2008 recession, and now also stands at around a quarter of a million.[71] When considering how Britain should respond to European and international migrants coming to the UK, we could do a lot worse than consider our own expectations of how we would hope be treated in Spain or the UAE.

Let's start with Spain; what we might call the 'Costa test'. Right now I would expect to be able to travel to Spain, get a job, live, work, and generally make a life there without needing formal permission from anyone. This is one of the basic principles of the European Union and applies for as long as both countries continue to be members. I would expect to be able to buy a house, drive a car, and generally do all the things that Spanish people can legally do. Culturally the differences are not massive by global standards. My expectations and habits might cause a few wry laughs or raised eyebrows, but I'm unlikely to be arrested for living a British lifestyle if that is (rather perversely) what I continue to do. If I got sick I would expect to use a Spanish doctor or hospital, and if I went out there with my family I would expect to be able to put my children in a Spanish school.

This comes with a few conditions of course. My children would have all their lessons in Spanish and would eventually take Spanish exams. I would not expect the Spanish authorities to lay on classes in English just for us; if I wanted my children to continue in the British education system then I would expect to pay for an international school out of my own pocket. If I lost my job I would not expect the Spanish state to support me. If my dream of a life in the sun does not work out the way I planned it then ultimately I am still a British citizen and it is my own nation that I would expect to fall back on in my time of need. Likewise if I could find only poorly paid work, I would not expect the Spanish government to make up the difference with welfare payments to give me a better standard of living. This would change if I was eventually accepted as a Spanish citizen. If I ever reached the point of formally deciding to identify myself with another nation (marriage could be one reason, cultural integration might be another)[72] then I become part of that nation 'for better and for worse, for richer for poorer, in sickness and in health'.

The 'Emirates test' will inevitably be a bit more stringent. Our two nations are not part of any international political union, and my right to live there will be subject to the decision of the UAE government. They will accept me as a worker because they want my skills, not because of any aspirations I may have. Once living there I am essentially a guest, and my expectations will be based on how I would expect a guest to be treated. I would certainly expect to be able to work in my professional field, earn a living, and generally get on with life without interference. I would not expect to have any kind of state-funded services available to me, which would mean arranging my own health insurance and schooling. I would expect to provide for my own needs, and if my job finished I would automatically assume that I would return home unless I could find alternative employment.

Our cultures are very different and I would expect to respect that. The UAE has a Muslim Arab culture, and things like drinking alcohol, immodest dress, and overt displays of affection are not permitted in public. None of these things infringe any fundamental freedoms; if I simply can't live without drinking in the street or making out on the beach then perhaps life in the UAE is not for me. I would hope to enjoy the freedom to practise my own religion and express my views as a private individual without suffering any harmful consequences. The distinction will be a fine one, and one where the reciprocity principle of mutual respect is at its most powerful.

If this is what I and probably the majority of British people would expect for ourselves when living and working in other countries, then it should similarly form the basis of what we offer to those coming to live and work in the UK. You can't pass a law requiring people to 'do unto others as you would have them do unto you'. But you can create a system for handling immigration and community cohesion which embodies those principles in practice. And when we do, maybe the attitudes which seek to blame all of society's problems on the outsider will slowly begin to fade.

The right stuff

The United Nations Declaration of Human Rights was signed in 1948. Forged in the unimaginable horror of two world wars, it identified fundamental rights that no human being should be denied. Its 30 articles guarantee freedom from slavery, torture, and persecution; freedom of conscience, religion, and expression; and access to the basic necessities of life. If observed it would mean that events such as the holocaust, the oppression of nations by totalitarian governments, and the suffering and death of the world's poor could never happen again.

In 2011, the then British Home Secretary Theresa May found herself at the centre of a media storm after claiming in a speech that an illegal immigrant had avoided deportation on human rights grounds because he owned a pet cat. The truth turned out to be slightly more complex: the Bolivian national in question was claiming that he should not be deported because he lived with his girlfriend and sending him back would infringe his right to family life. Shared ownership of Maya the cat was one of several factors cited in evidence to prove the strength of their relationship. His appeal was granted, although the judgement was actually given on non-feline technical grounds relating to a failure by the authorities to follow proper procedures, hence the controversy.

The case was just one in a long series featuring individuals attempting to use human rights laws to overturn some aspect of a judgement or decision which had been given against them. The result has been a steady erosion of trust in the very idea of human rights itself. For many people, the concept that started as a visionary attempt to elevate humanity has now been reduced to a playground for overpaid lawyers and unrepentant criminals looking for loopholes to escape justice.

The first problem with human rights is that they are impotent unless someone takes action to implement them. You cannot eat a right to food, a right to shelter will not keep you warm, and a right to freedom of expression does not seemingly prevent you from being fired from your public sector job for 'saying the wrong thing'. The second is that where they are written into laws and constitutions, they are most easily used by individuals who have something to gain at the expense of society at large. So a right to family life can be asserted in the courts as a tactic to fight against a deportation order, but offers no practical help at all to a mother of young children whose partner has just abandoned her.

For most of human history the concept of rights barely existed. People were defined by their responsibilities towards each other. These could be moral obligations, legal duties, or those created by the structures of communities and societies. Responsibilities gave practical expression to a set of relational values which at times were helpful and beneficial (responsibility to help the poor and needy) and at other times simply reinforced existing power structures (responsibility to defer to your social superiors). Declarations of rights offer a template to challenge us to live up to those responsibilities, but they cannot replace them. Human rights will only ever be observed to the extent that human responsibilities are exercised.

A right to family life will exist in practice when a responsibility to protect and promote family life is accepted by the community, the state, and the market. Communities must nurture and protect families and fight against the culture of selfishness and consumerist attitudes to relationships which tears them apart. The state must implement policies which reflect a responsibility to promote the wellbeing of families and children, testing its decisions in other areas to ensure that this responsibility is not overlooked. And markets must be constructed (and if necessary regulated) in such a way as to accept this responsibility as one of the outputs they are required to deliver.

The same is true of all other human rights. On their own they are noble but impotent. When implemented directly as legal rights, they become open to abuse and yet remain ineffective for many who need them most. Only when comprehensively expressed as a network of responsibilities can they actually deliver their promise and potential to serve the wellbeing of every human being.

Open doors

Given their obvious potential for good, how can it be that tolerance, human rights, and equality have become offensive concepts to so many people? To be sure, a small minority are just viciously and wilfully prejudiced. But there are plenty of people who are capable of great kindness, empathy, and generosity, yet still express real anger whenever the issue of immigration is mentioned. What can drive someone who obviously has many of the qualities of a good neighbour to be so sternly opposed to one particular section of their community?

Most of us will admit that our worst qualities come out when we feel threatened or imposed upon. Successive governments have inadvertently treated the population in exactly this way. The last half century has seen the largest sustained period of immigration in British history[73] without any direct popular mandate or consent. The law has often been portrayed as being on the side of those who abuse the system rather than those who play by the rules. Multiculturalism has exaggerated the negative aspects by encouraging communities to retain separate identities and live apart from one another. A culture of enforced tolerance has given people the impression that they have no choices, and political correctness has prevented them from expressing their fears and grievances. But it does seem clear that the same people who react negatively under fear or threat will respond very differently when they feel things are done with their control and consent. The shift is from an ethic of rights and tolerance to one of hospitality.

Hospitality is something which is offered voluntarily. It is based on the generosity of the giver, not the rights of the recipient. It retains a distinction between the two while allowing a relationship to form between them. It can afford to be open and welcoming because it retains an element of control and cannot be imposed. If (as happened during the evacuations of the Second World War) I was told by government edict that I had to put up strangers in my house, I might respond by making excuses or grudgingly doing the minimum possible. When I receive guests of my own free choice I offer a welcome that is generous and genuine. One of the most remarkable features of the Syrian refugee crisis in 2015 was the sudden surge of individuals and communities pro-actively offering their own home or town as a sanctuary for families fleeing war and chaos. While any sign of the government weakening border controls was greeted with howls of protest, these spontaneous expressions of openness and hospitality received a generally positive reaction.

Converting this organic expression of hospitality into a coherent response requires some brave and radical policy decisions. The inherent problem with a centralised approach to receiving refugees is that the benefits are broad and long-term (we affirm that compassion remains an important aspect of our national identity and strengthen our international reputation and clout), but the challenges are local and immediate (pressures on housing, employment, schools, health services and community cohesion). If the areas which are targeted for resettlement believe that they will be personally disadvantaged as a result, they are likely to respond with anger and hostility. And yet the paradox remains that people continue spontaneously to offer themselves and their communities, despite knowing that they would also experience these same impacts.

Hospitality can only be offered, not demanded. Instead of requisitioning housing and assigning regional quotas, governments should enable individuals and communities to make good on their promises of hospitality by allowing the funding to follow the offers. If those who are making themselves available to welcome refugees were directly provided with the resources to do so, social attitudes to resettlement would be transformed. Households who opened their doors to refugees would receive a direct financial benefit to offset the costs (financial and personal) that they incur. Localities would be funded for the additional public services that are needed.

Although the main motive for hospitality is not financial, the truth-telling power of the market will enable us to determine the price at which people are willing and able to follow through sustainably on their good intentions.[74]

Instead of finding themselves isolated in ghettoes surrounded by fear and resentment, the new arrivals would now immediately start on the journey of healing and community integration. Sceptics would almost certainly be surprised by the breadth and depth of response that would be released. And if we do reach the end of our reserves of hospitality, that is about the most authentic indication possible that our national capacity to accept refugees has been reached. There will eventually be a limit, and discerning it by matching off the available offers of community hospitality is a far more powerful approach than setting national targets, which are nothing more than poorly informed political guesswork.

Hospitality extends beyond our own front door. A hospitable attitude to my neighbours means that I share relationships and life with them. A hospitable attitude to workmates means being open to relationships that go beyond the purely professional. Both will help to grow and reinforce the network of wellbeing-promotion in the community as a whole. It also has relevance in many areas beyond those relating purely to immigration. Our treatment of excluded young people, the isolated elderly, homeless people, and ex-offenders all have the potential to be transformed by the same community-led, hospitality-inspired approach to meeting social needs.

Politicians can create the right conditions and offer leadership, but they cannot force communities to adopt hospitable attitudes. In this chapter we have placed a heavy reliance on the community as an actor, to build positive relationships across what have traditionally been seen as boundaries and flashpoints. Weakened as it is by the relentless advance of market forces and state institutions, is the community actually in a position to carry this burden? And if not, what, if anything, can be done to strengthen it?

8

OPEN THE COMMUNITY CHEST

There is no such thing as society ...

Margaret Thatcher

... There is living tapestry of men and women and people and the beauty of that tapestry and the quality of our lives will depend upon how much each of us is prepared to take responsibility for ourselves and each of us is prepared to turn round and help by our own efforts those who are unfortunate.

Margaret Thatcher

For many years I spent my Thursday evenings driving a double-decker bus. As well as being a British cultural icon and the fulfilment of a slightly childish ambition (what little boy doesn't secretly want to be a bus or train driver?), this particular bus was special because inside it is kitted out as a fully equipped mobile youth centre. Every week, a team of volunteers faithfully takes it up to our local park and for a few hours in the evening it provides somewhere for teenagers to hang out, play video games, drink tea (even juvenile delinquents drink tea in Britain), and maybe find a listening ear and a place to talk or pray about their problems.

The bus has no 'official' funding, and is just one example of the kind of community project which goes on every week in towns across the length and breadth of the country. It is operated by

Bar'n'bus trust; a small charity based in nearby Southend-on-Sea who hit on the idea about 20 years ago and have been gradually expanding it ever since. The volunteers who operate it are drawn from local churches, who also pay the day-to-day running costs. A rota of volunteer drivers move the bus to and from its base at the beginning and end of the night, and most of us also then stay to chat with the kids for the evening. Leftover cakes and bread are donated by a nearby bakery. The local police are regular visitors, and in our first year we observed relationships improve from the kids 'doing a runner' when the police turned up to a willingness to at least stay and chat and learn each other's names.

For a few young people the bus has been life changing. Just having someone to listen and encourage them is something which they themselves identify as having helped them to get through their troubled teenage years. For the rest, it provides that essential 'something to do' which they look forward to every Thursday. In the first year of operation, the level of reported minor and nuisance crime in our town on bus nights dropped by 34%. The probable perpetrators were still being a minor nuisance, but were now doing so in an environment where things wouldn't get out of hand (mostly).

All being well

The volunteers who work on the Corringham bar'n'bus worry that their achievements are small when set against the backdrop of need amongst young people in our town. On one level they may be right (it is 'only' a few hours a week), but in wellbeing terms they are having a positive effect at multiple levels.

Crime is reduced: that makes the entire community feel safer. Young people have a chance to build positive relationships with their friends in an environment where bullying and abuse are confronted and challenged. They also start to form relationships of openness and trust with adults: something many of them do not always experience at home. The bus provides at least one part of their social life which is drug and alcohol free: this opens them up to choices that could significantly improve their health and life chances later on. It gives them real-world role models: not the celebrity kind, but ordinary people like them who have steady jobs, stable marriages, and seem to be enjoying life and doing well as a result. Just that one personal connection can lead to a step change in aspirations and their chance of making it through education and into the world of work. There are benefits for the volunteers too. Their own relationships are deepened by serving together, and their perceptions of the world and sense of empowerment to affect it will be far different from those who just sit at home watching another documentary about troubled teens.

The community as an actor is at its most powerful when it is released to deliver the relational aspects of wellbeing. The market is blind to relationships unless they involve people as buyers, sellers, producers, or consumers. The state can neither legislate for them nor commission them.[75] But as we have seen, the actions of market and state do affect them both positively and negatively.

People desire relationships. They want friendship, they want family, and they want community. And unlike the desire for more material stuff which generally fails to deliver on its promises, those who have more and better relationships do consistently report higher levels of life satisfaction and wellbeing. Like a plant reaching towards the light, communities will naturally grow and flourish in relational terms when the conditions are right. To build relational wellbeing, we need to ensure that those conditions are created and protected. Clear the ground for community to grow and it will do so. Choke it out or make the conditions dry and infertile and it will wither. The question for policy makers has to be: what are the conditions in which relationships flourish, and how can we promote them in practice?

Get knotted

The relationships which matter the most to us are the closest and most intimate ones. As we saw earlier, married couples enjoy higher levels of life satisfaction than any other group. Cohabiting couples come next, followed by single people. Those who have experienced the pain of separation or divorce experience the lowest levels of life satisfaction as a group.[76] When combined with the fact that parents of children experience higher life satisfaction, it does seem that the stereotype of married family life as a desirable social aspiration is well justified by the evidence.

When asked about their hopes and dreams for the future, a remarkable 80–90% of young people will state that their aim is to find a partner, get married, and remain with that person for life.[77] While these aspirations have not changed much down the years, the chances of fulfilling them clearly have. The number of marriages taking place in the UK has fallen by a third since 1970, despite a rising population. Around 95% of today's pensioners have experienced married life, but it is projected that only 75% of their children and grandchildren will do so. The changes occurred in two distinct phases. Divorce rates rose rapidly in the 1960 and 1970s, but have largely stabilised since. In the 1980s and 1990s, the trend was for more couples living together without getting married. This change is clearly reflected in the types of families that children are born into. In 1980, just 12% of children were born to unmarried parents. By 2009 that number had risen to nearly 50%, due almost entirely to the growth in unmarried couples.

This clearly represents social and cultural change on a historically unprecedented scale, but the question is 'Does it matter?' There is a growing body of evidence to suggest that it matters a great deal. Based on the simple criteria of personal wellbeing statistics, the fewer people who fulfil their youthful ambition to get and stay married, the less content we will be as a society. If this simple correlation was not enough, the effects of relationship breakdown and especially family breakdown are often catastrophic. Children raised in broken families of various types are on average: poorer; less well educated; less healthy; more likely to commit or experience crime; more likely to suffer mental health problems, neglect, abuse, or addiction; and less likely to find decent employment. They go on to experience poorer relationships themselves as adults; greater levels of domestic violence; higher rates of teenage pregnancy; and their own family units are themselves more likely to subsequently break up. Thankfully this is not true in every case; there is always hope, but statistically the odds are heavily stacked against you.

All of these problems come at a massive cost to the individuals involved and to society as a whole. The costs appear in every welfare office, housing department, job centre, hospital, and police force who find themselves dealing directly or indirectly with the consequences. They currently run at £20–£24 billion per year. And because unmarried families are much more likely to break up, it is here that the problems are mostly concentrated. Married couples still account for over half of all births, but go on to suffer just 20% of the splits and 14% of the costs. The 'other 50%' of unmarried parents experience 80% of the splits and incur 86% of all the costs. The main cause of family crisis is not divorce, but the failure of other forms of relationship. Half of children born to unmarried parents will see them split up before their fifth birthday. If the parents were married, 11 out of 12 will still be together.

The biggest single loss of fathers in British history occurred during the First World War. It is estimated that 500,000 children lost their father during the four years of conflict.[78] The social consequences were felt for decades. Today, around 350,000 children every year 'lose' their fathers to family breakup.[79] That's nearly three times the annual rate experienced during the bloodiest war in history, and there is no sign of a ceasefire anywhere in sight. If that comparison sounds too dramatic, then consider the hard statistics. According to the UK ONS survey, the effect of separation or divorce on individual wellbeing is actually worse than bereavement.[80] Historians may well look back and identify the late twentieth and early twenty-first centuries primarily as a period of social crisis; the great breakdown of family relationships.

Successive governments have recognised the problem but seemed powerless to stop the trend. It is neither practicable nor desirable for governments to try and control who should marry or split up. The market has offered no answers either. Relationships themselves are not tradable commodities, despite the size and power of the contemporary wedding and divorce industries. So what, if anything, can be done to reverse this damaging crisis?

The good news is that, as we have seen, people do still long for stable, committed, long-term relationships. What people say they want and what will reduce the levels of distress, damage, and cost in society as a whole are still basically pulling in the same direction. It has been suggested that the idea of commitment has three dimensions to it, and is strongest when all three are present:[81]

'*Structural*' *commitment*: external pressures such as financial factors or social expectations which encourage people to stay together;

'*Moral*' *commitment*: a personal conviction that remaining together is the 'right thing to do', often driven by cultural or religious values;

'*Personal*' *commitment*: a desire to stay together because it is satisfying and pleasurable to do so.

People are most likely to fulfil their relational aspirations, and to experience the wellbeing benefits which normally result, when all three dimensions are actively encouraged. We will now look at each of these dimensions in turn and consider what can be done to promote them.

Calling shotgun

Structural commitment is the area which the state is most likely to be able to influence. A brief examination shows that, far from structurally encouraging commitment, government policies have created a situation where exactly the opposite behaviour is rewarded in practice.

Even successful, prosperous couples raising families are subtly penalised by the tax system. Two members of a couple with no children might expect to have similar earning potential, everything else being equal. Where one parent then chooses to take on home-making and childcare responsibilities, it is likely that they will either give up paid employment or work part time. This is a personal decision, but it comes at a considerable tax penalty. Two average earners in the UK will expect to pay just over 20% of their combined income in tax. A couple making the same total amount where one works and the other is a full-time parent will pay nearer 30%.[82]

For couples on low incomes or dependent on state welfare payments, the discrepancy is even greater. While wages and taxes are paid per individual, benefits for both working and unemployed people are calculated per household based on need. A household consisting of a couple with children will receive slightly more than a single parent (they have one extra person to feed and clothe), but the difference is actually quite small. Most of the costs (housing, heating, bills, supporting children) are similar whether the household has one parent or two. Looked at the other way, if you split up you will receive a big increase in total combined welfare payments from the state. We already saw this issue in the area of social housing, where family breakdown is one of the ways to get to the 'front of the queue'. The same issue also shows up in the benefits system. Whether you are unemployed or in low paid work, you are financially better off apart than together. And when money is tight, that really matters. It matters much more than to the middle class family, who may complain about the injustices of the tax system but experience little real hardship as a result.

At worst the 'couple penalty' built into our welfare systems encourages outright fraud. If an unemployed couple split up, they will be given an additional home and extra income to ensure their basic needs are met. If they then get back together, the temptation to keep claiming the higher level of benefits and even to rent out the 'spare' property for cash can be overwhelming. In one case reported in Thurrock in 2009, a woman narrowly avoided jail after over-claiming £11,000 in this way.[83] No-one is condoning benefit fraud, but it is sobering to realise that we have created a society where someone can be taken to court for getting back together with their estranged husband.

Even where people play by the rules, those rules cost them dear. Entire sections of society find themselves financially penalised for getting together and staying together. These are exactly the same sections of society (those dependent fully or partly on state benefits and/or living in social housing) who also experience the highest levels of relationship breakdown, unmarried parenthood, and of co-habitation as opposed to marriage. This is unlikely to be a coincidence.

If we are looking to reinforce structural commitment, we are going about it in spectacularly the wrong way. The most obvious step that governments could take to support durable family relationships would be to end the 'couple penalty' in the tax and welfare systems. There are already plenty of detailed policy proposals for doing so: greater transferable tax allowances for married couples, a couple premium in the welfare system to recognise the lower social costs and better outcomes achieved by stable families, and so on. While we are at it, it would be helpful to change a legal system which makes divorce lawyers mandatory but relationship counsellors optional, and pays the former ten times more per hour than the latter.

One of the reasons that governments have been slow to implement these seemingly obvious measures is said to be cost. However, what we are talking about is a system which already discriminates financially against couples and families. Re-balancing it would inevitably mean that those not in these situations received a slightly smaller share of the pie, but eliminating a discriminatory penalty can hardly be argued as 'unfair'. The real political problem is not lack of cash, but lack of courage.

One thing that may be making governments more timid than they should be in this area is the effect of political correctness. Over the last decade or so, we have seen a gradual removal of all language relating to marriage from official documents and statistics. Where we used to talk of husbands, wives, and spouses, the term 'partner' has gradually taken over. It is increasingly impossible to indicate marital status accurately on many government forms; you are asked to confirm whether you are 'in a marriage or living with someone as if you were married'. Ignoring the comedy potential of attempting to explain what 'living with someone as if you were married' actually means, we have inadvertently removed another of the key drivers to structural commitment. If even the government is so embarrassed by the idea of marriage that it refuses to mention it in public, it is hardly surprising that people feel no sense of social pressure to formalise their relationships.

One excuse sometimes used is that to overtly refer to marriage might be considered discriminatory against those in other forms of relationships or none. This is a sweeping assumption which is almost never tested with the supposed victims of the discrimination. When you do ask, inevitably the answer is that people are very happy for married couples to openly declare their relationship status. Those whose relationships have broken up do not resent the idea of successful marriage, and statistically many in fact will subsequently go on to re-marry themselves. Suppressing marriage from public view does not reassure other groups, it actually threatens them (if marrieds can be discriminated against, then what chance do I stand?). So long as other relationship statuses are appropriately and sensitively recognised, there is no problem with marriage being given clear and overt recognition too.

In the case of statistics, the problem is even more pressing. As we have seen, the differences in outcomes for married and unmarried families are enormous. Yet for years, governments have collected data on the basis of 'married or living together' as if these options were identical. Whether by accident or design, the catastrophic social problems that have taken hold disproportionately among families of unmarried parents have been hidden from view because policy makers tried to pretend that they were one and the same thing.

The final structural driver working against commitment is the early sexualisation of relationships, especially among children and young people. Traditionally British society had a strong expectation of progressive relationship development which ran: dating, courtship, engagement, marriage, sex, children. Significant social pressure was applied to comply with this model, even if it was ignored more often than those communities liked to admit. Today, the term 'girlfriend' can be used to mean anything from someone you have been on a second date with to someone you have lived with for ten years and had three children with. It is hardly surprising that young people who are less emotionally mature struggle to identify levels of commitment in relationships. Relationships move from low commitment to high physical commitment very quickly, with the intermediate steps of developing emotional, practical, and mutual commitment missed out altogether. This provides a very poor foundation for durable relationships and no relational narrative to progress towards marriage.

The response in healthcare and education has not helped children to develop relationally either. The drive to tackle the obvious negative effects of early sexual activity (underage pregnancy and sexually transmitted diseases) has led to earlier and more explicit sex education and an emphasis on 'safe sex' as the social imperative. Schools in Thurrock will not administer a headache tablet without direct parental involvement, but may hand out condoms freely and entirely confidentially to children who are below the legal age of sexual consent.[84] These approaches can deliver short-term results amongst sexually active teens (i.e. they can reduce pregnancy and infection rates at a particular time and place), but come at the cost of creating a long-term culture of earlier and more frequent sex. The net effect is that overall outcomes have continued to get worse, even while individual programmes have been able to claim 'success' among their particular target groups. With the media following this lead and portraying sexual activity primarily as a matter of personal choice, the weakening of structural commitment has accelerated rapidly.

Changing this culture to one which provides appropriate drivers towards structural commitment requires a new approach to leadership. Authorities need to be seen defending the rationale behind protective measures such as a legal age of consent, and not deliberately using public money to help children break the law with impunity. The current approach makes the law a mockery, and conveys the message that obeying it is a matter of choice. Education should focus on communicating the information clearly. Children need to understand the facts about pregnancy and sexually transmitted diseases without it being implied that practising 'safe sex' is the only response that society expects from them. The reality that marriage and family remains an aspirational goal for a clear majority should be strongly and positively affirmed.[85] Remedial measures such as condom distribution may still be appropriate for some groups, but it is important that this does not become visibly identified with institutions such as schools and public services which are supposed to represent authority. Teenagers will continue to push the boundaries; that's what they do. The role of society is to provide and enforce those boundaries, not dismantle them to make the process of rebellion easier. The journey into adulthood defined as moving from challenging the rules to owning and defending them is especially important for young men. Lack of anything solid to rebel against at one end or anything aspirational to earn your place in at the other end fatally hinders this process, and consigns young people to perpetual relational adolescence.

Moral majority

Moral commitment based on personally held religious or ethical values has to come from the individual. The main difference between structural and moral commitment is that structural commitment is demanded by society whereas moral commitment is expressed whether society expects it or not. Pretty much all of the great world religions promote faithful commitment in the context of marriage. You would thus expect that liberal democracies, which tend to claim religious freedom as one of their own values, would find it easy (and expedient) to affirm moral commitment as a positive outcome of freely held personal beliefs. The reality has been slightly different.

In contrast to previous generations, it has become fashionable to represent religious or moral beliefs as a matter of private, personal conviction. This view makes it legitimate to hold pretty much any belief system imaginable (back to the problem of indiscriminate tolerance), provided that its outworkings are confined to the private sphere. This would be fine, except that almost none of the world's religions see it that way. Christianity is not just the principal spiritual and religious tradition of the British Isles, it is also deeply woven into our social, cultural, and political fabric too. Our Christian forebears took a leading role in building democracy, abolishing slavery, challenging poverty, reforming prisons, providing education and healthcare, cancelling third world debt, and a myriad other things besides. The idea that Christianity can be restricted to a matter of private belief would have been completely alien to them, and is equally foreign to most of the other world religions too.

In adopting a position that personal beliefs are valid but that they should not be allowed to influence the public sphere, society risks cutting off one of its greatest historical sources of strength. Everyone has beliefs and values whether they are religious or not. The version of 'secular neutrality' where religious values are excluded on principle is just a transparent attempt to promote secular worldviews above spiritual ones. True secular neutrality means that ideas are judged on merit whatever belief system they originate from.

The benefits of moral commitment as a positive social force are easily and objectively demonstrated from evidence. This means that society should allow it to be advocated and promoted, not as a grudging requirement of religious tolerance but as a valued contribution to social policy. In a secular democracy the state does not get involved in promoting religion per se, but it can and should allow religious insights which lead to policies or initiatives beneficial to wellbeing to be advocated and adopted. Too often, state institutions have starved faith-based community initiatives of legitimacy and funding on spurious grounds of equality, diversity, or tolerance. Instead of encouraging all parts of the community to make a positive contribution, we have come close to adopting a position where no-one can contribute unless their beliefs conform to some kind of post-modern, politically correct script. The fact that a particular group encourages moral commitment is not an automatic reason to support their work with cash or other resources, but it should clearly count in their favour when decisions are being made.

All you need is love

While structural commitment and moral commitment have found themselves under attack, personal commitment has suffered from a massive burden of over-expectation. The general social trend towards individualism and consumerism has seen relationships become represented as the ultimate lifestyle accessory. They are the dominant theme of our popular music, fashion, leisure activities, films, and literature. Our culture idealises relationships as a means of personal fulfilment, and has created multi-billion pound industries to help people pursue them, directly or indirectly. The result is that people repeatedly give up on relationships, not always because they are inherently bad but because they do not match the hyped and distorted expectations which have been sold with them.

Wellbeing data shows that marriage and family life do indeed lead to higher levels of fulfilment and life satisfaction. It also shows that couples and parents are just as likely as anyone else to suffer stress, anxiety, and problems day to day. Traditional marriage vows express a commitment that is 'for better for worse, for richer for poorer, in sickness and in health, 'til death us do part'. Personal commitment, defined as commitment based on the expectation of personal pleasure and satisfaction from the relationship, is 'for better, for richer, in health, 'til I cease to enjoy it or get a better offer'. A relationship based entirely on structural and moral commitment would be dull and dutiful, but one based purely on personal commitment is selfish and fickle.

Only the community with its network of relationships and opinion formers can challenge the idea that commitment should be restricted to 'only putting in what I get out'. Every voice will play a part, including media figures, educationalists, celebrities, business and community leaders, and public officials. Political leaders do not have a monopoly or even a controlling stake in cultural leadership, but nor can they abdicate their role entirely. In the past, policy makers and implementers have been complicit with the idea that relationships can be defined purely in terms of personal choices and consumerist outcomes. We must change our public language and value statements to restore a balanced view of commitment that has personal, structural, and moral dimensions. This at least can be implemented as a practical policy goal, and will kick-start the long process of restoring the balance that has been lost.

Das capital

While relationships and families are a key building block of community, they are not the whole story. A society consisting only of strong, committed family units who remained locked behind their own front doors and never engaged with their neighbours would be no kind of community at all.

Politically, the idea that people coming together at community level to engage with one another, form relationships, and solve problems seems to have pretty much universal support. On the left there is a deep attachment to concepts like 'co-operative' and 'social solidarity'. On the right, there is a similar value placed on 'civil society' or the 'little platoons' of voluntary endeavour. Given that such a broad consensus exists around the importance of community groups and organisations (if not the terminology used to describe them), it is surprising that the actual level of participation in such groups has been falling year on year.

In my own life I have been personally involved with churches and Christian groups, political activism and party membership, local and international poverty alleviation, voluntary youthwork, community arts, and the boy scouts.[86] Some of the groups I have been part of have grown while others no longer exist, but overall voluntary and community groups in the UK have been experiencing a relentless decline in membership. To give just two examples, membership of the main British political parties has declined from 3 million in the 1960s to 400,000 today, and weekly church attendance has halved in the last 30 years. The only mass membership organisations which seem to be bucking the trend are groups such as the RSPB and National Trust.[87] It is telling that these organisations do not generally expect any form of direct participation or involvement from their 'members'. Instead they sell access to their facilities and services as 'membership benefits' on what is basically a consumer model with a dash of added social purpose. Our own membership of the National Trust is based primarily on an economic calculation that it will save us on admission and parking charges to various family days out in the course of a year (and they also send us a nice magazine).

This decline is of more than academic interest. Although numbers have been falling steadily, still 25% of people in England report that they volunteer formally at least once a month.[88] Areas such as youthwork, support for the elderly, and charitable fundraising are especially dependent on church[89] and voluntary groups, and provision in these areas would virtually collapse if the community element were to disappear. In wellbeing terms, we saw that one of the key differences between high wellbeing nations and low wellbeing ones is the level of collective participation in community activities. On this measure, Britain is slipping steadily down the league table of relational wellbeing, and in some areas has probably already been relegated to the lower division.

This rich asset base of community groups and activity is sometimes referred to as 'social capital'. And while it remains a vitally important part of our national balance sheet, we seem to have been in 'social recession' year after year. Why is this happening, and what can be done to restore it to growth?

The big retreat

Going back a century or two, the majority of community services in the UK were provided by churches and voluntary groups. This included many things that we would today recognise as formal public services (education, healthcare, and the alleviation of poverty) and also public service in the broader sense (work with young, elderly and vulnerable people and in the areas of arts, culture, and community life). Their great strength was that they were local, organic, flexible, and had strong relational connections to their communities. Their weaknesses were a vulnerability to being disrupted or overwhelmed by rapid social change, patchy coverage, and the fact that they tended to be weakest in the areas of greatest social need such as fast-growing industrial towns and cities. Social capital can take generations to build, and can be difficult to transplant into new environments.

The emergence of the modern welfare state set universal basic standards that applied everywhere. It also brought virtually all new and existing provision under direct state control. Public spending became a major part of the economy, increasing from less than 20% at the start of the twentieth century to over 40% for most of the post-war period. This in turn led to a mass marketisation of community services. Not only do public services themselves follow most of the day-to-day principles of markets (they hire labour, buy materials, purchase buildings, and so on), there has also been a steady increase in the number of services bought directly from the market by government.

Where the state and market advance, community tends to retreat. In addition to the direct transfer of community institutions into the state sector at the birth of the welfare state, one of the effects of the culture of universal welfare has been to move the sense of responsibility from the community to the state and the market. People are generally less willing to provide things for themselves or their neighbours if they are seen as a state entitlement or a traded commodity. All the while that sharing childcare responsibilities is a social norm, it is moderated by a network of mutual support and obligations. Once it becomes something that is provided by state funded nurseries or private childminders and daycare centres, asking your neighbours or family to do it feels like demanding a freebie.

In addition to being 'crowded out' by the state and market, the voluntary, community, and faith sector has also been subtly discriminated against in the allocation of public monies. Even after community services had been largely taken over by the state and operated on market principles, you would expect that community groups would still be in a strong position to 'bid' for the work. They continue to have deep relational links which they can leverage, and on average bring in an additional £2 or £3 of charitable donations for every pound of state funding they receive. These are real and tangible advantages, but they are ones which 'fair' public procurement rules are deliberately blind to. Buyers of public services are pretty much obliged to ignore the additional benefits which their funding could produce, focusing instead on the narrow market transaction of price per unit of service. This puts power in the hands of large organisations which can mass produce services as commodities, at the expense of community groups which deliver them in a more relational and holistic way. That's fine if you are emptying bins or manufacturing surgical equipment, but it has led to a degradation in the real value of many welfare services which deal with people not products.

Finally, a growing culture of political correctness in the public sector has made it more and more difficult for values-based organisations, especially faith groups, to serve their communities in line with their own distinctive ethos. The stated values of diversity and tolerance would seem to provide a firm basis for including faith groups and other strongly values-based organisations, who are often the most likely to attract and inspire people to get involved.[90] But in reality, 'equality and diversity' has frequently been used as a reason for excluding these groups rather than working with them. They have been faced with a culture in officialdom which is suspicious of their values and motives and fails to understand their language. It also expects to see a hard dividing wall between belief and action, which is the exact opposite of why most of these groups choose to get involved in community service in the first place.

Turning the Tide

To end the social recession and start a renaissance of community action, these recessionary pressures need to be eliminated. The public sector can and should recognise the additional value that community groups can bring, and start working with them in ways which formally acknowledge these extra benefits. Public contracts need to be placed in a way which recognises natural community boundaries. There is little point placing an area-wide contract if all of the capable community providers are operating in individual localities; they will be excluded through lack of scale before the process has even started. Tenders need to ask the right questions about the additional community benefits that can be offered beyond the basic service, and fair and transparent ways for putting a value on these devised. Equality and diversity has to mean exactly what it says: that groups with beliefs that differ from the politically correct doctrines of the public sector are given a fair and equal chance to participate.

While releasing organisations will help enormously, there is also work to be done on helping individuals to volunteer. The idea that volunteers are tied up in bureaucracy, red tape, and health and safety legislation has become a stereotype, but it does contain a considerable element of truth. Everything in life is a tradeoff between cost and benefit, risk and reward. We have gone so far to eliminate every last risk that we have lost many of the rewards that come from an active, involved community. Volunteers should be protected when they act with reasonable care and good intent, not sued the moment anything goes wrong because they have not filled in all of the correct forms.

We also need to understand and respond to the financial factors that motivate and enable community action. Volunteers do not expect to be paid a wage for what they do. They are giving of their time and skills for reasons other then the need to earn an income, and to seek to pay them a wage would actually invalidate their real motives. At the same time, many of them would have the option of doing part-time work instead and could benefit from some form of financial recognition. This is especially true where they are giving not just a couple of hours a week but maybe the equivalent of entire days. Young and older volunteers and those not in paid employment often fall into this category. The ability for a charity to pay a student or recent retiree 'generous expenses' or some kind of small honorarium can sometimes feel appropriate, and represent a fair and honourable position for both parties. Trying to do this in practice while achieving compliance with tax and expenses law, minimum wage and equal pay legislation, employment protection law, and so on is nigh on impossible. The rules are simply not written for this type of arrangement, but they have become so all encompassing that they often apply whether those involved want them to or not. There is an urgent need to simplify the law for semi-voluntary work, to enable charities and individuals to make small amounts go a long way by mutual consent.

Pesos and say-sos

Statistically, one of the most deprived areas in Thurrock is the port town of Tilbury. Over the years, there have been several well-funded government initiatives aimed at achieving community regeneration. Much of the money has ended up being paid to external consultants and project managers with no particular knowledge or insight into the local area. Some has gone to support new projects or renovate buildings. But when the initiatives finished and the funding moved on, we have rarely had much of any lasting value to show for all their efforts. The social problems still remain, and there is a sense that what has been attempted was done 'to' the community rather than 'with' them.

Public funding for community projects is generally allocated by a long and tortuous process of applications. One set of government officials set strategic priorities and allocate pots of money for various types of initiatives that might deliver them. Another set of officials at local level, often working with representatives of charities and community groups, then spend weeks filling in application forms to claim the cash and put it to work. What generally ensues is an endless game of 'pin the project on the funding'. If your real aim is urban regeneration but the flavour of the month is green transport, you will end up building smart new cycle paths and bus shelters. If the money then switches into youth and children you will re-equip the playground or refurbish the youth centre, and so on. This happens regardless of whether those particular initiatives were actually the main priorities or not. From the government's perspective, the money is rarely used efficiently for the stated purposes (despite reams of post-project reports and benefit statements 'proving' that it was). And at community level, the conditions that come with funding are at best a hindrance and at worst a serious distraction. Many groups have had their focus dragged away from what they are actually good at and passionate about, into chasing after whatever they can currently get funding for.

At the other end of the scale, the largest charitable institutions have a very high level of control over priorities in their chosen field of work. Since 1994, the Bill and Melinda Gates Foundation (set up by multi-billionaire Bill Gates) has contributed around £10 billion into the field of public health in poorer countries. So large is the power of the Gates foundation that their key priorities in areas such as tackling malaria, tuberculosis, and AIDS have become *the* priorities, not just for the foundation itself but for researchers, charities, and even governments, all of whom benefit from their funding. As philanthropist Sir Tom Hunter has said, 'he who has the pesos, has the say-so'.[91]

Smaller community-based charities are normally supported by individuals who have direct personal contact with them. They can see their results first hand, and will only continue to give if they are confident that their money is being well spent. This can make them highly effective at identifying and prioritising community needs and coming up with innovative, cost-effective solutions which make best use of local strengths and build on social capital. Given these advantages, it would be desirable if the same ability to 'steer' public policy and allocation of resources was available to community groups as is enjoyed by the largest charitable foundations.

One of the simplest ways to do so would be to offer match-funded tax relief on all donations to charitable community groups and projects. At present, adults in the UK give £11 billion per year to charities, to which the government adds about another £1 billion through income tax relief.[92] If eligible community-based charities were instead able to claim a 100% bonus, control of government spending on community activities would be placed directly into the hands of local donors.[93] The complex, distant, and often inefficient processes currently used for allocating funds would be replaced by a simple mechanism whereby local donors 'putting their money where their mouth is' got a real say on how cash for their community was spent. By transferring decision-making power from the state to the community, it will help to end the 'social recession' and bring a new vibrancy to voluntary and community groups, which will become better resourced and more directly able to control their own priorities.

People's Peers

The community has always suffered from having the lowest status of the three main actors. The state has power and the market has money; the community is fondly regarded but that doesn't necessarily secure it a seat at the top table. Some of the measures above would go a significant way towards ensuring the community sector is better financed. Providing more formal influence is tricky, but there is a constitutional 'opportunity' in twenty-first-century Britain which is wide open for a community-based solution.

The House of Lords feels like an anachronism in a modern democracy. Its function is to review, revise, and amend the decisions of the House of Commons (the elected bit of the British Parliament), but the fact that it is made up of establishment figures appointed by successive Prime Ministers (plus a handful of Bishops and a small residue of 'hereditary peers' from the surprisingly recent days when it still included members of the aristocracy by right) has robbed it of legitimacy and credibility.

Reform of the House of Lords seems to get discussed by every government in every decade, but so far no more radical changes have seen the light of day. One obvious answer is to move to a fully elected second chamber as used by many other democracies, but this has never happened for three reasons. Firstly, we already have an elected House of Commons, and electing the Lords as well could set up an unhealthy competition leading to confusion and deadlock. At the moment the Lords focus on scrutinising and (generally) improving the work of the Commons; if the Lords had the legitimacy of a separate electoral mandate then it would be far less clear who should take the lead. Secondly, trust and confidence in elected politicians generally is at a pretty low ebb, and it would be difficult to persuade people that more elections and more politicians is the answer to anything. And finally, despite its anachronistic composition, customs, and outfits, the House of Lords is quietly competent at what it does, and it is difficult to imagine any of the proposed alternatives doing a better job.

So far the argument seems to have revolved around the percentage of political appointees (lacking a democratic mandate but often bringing other valuable experiences and skills) versus elected peers (democratically legitimate but forever open to the accusation of being party stooges). What the Lords actually needs is an entirely different form of legitimacy; deriving not from the ballot box but from society itself.

Let's imagine a House of Lords which is appointed not by politicians and Prime Ministers, but by the deep reservoir of societies and organisations which make up the foundations of our civil society. Such a chamber would have immense credibility, produced partly by its broadly representative nature (it would include many highly regarded mass-membership organisations) and partly by its expertise (why would you not want medical or highways matters being debated by members of the Royal College of Surgeons or the Institution of Civil Engineers?). This legitimacy would be of an entirely different and complementary nature to the House of Commons, ensuring that a clash of functions remained unlikely.

Setting up such a chamber would be surprisingly easy. A Royal Commission would decide the composition of the new House of Lords. It would aim to achieve a balanced representation from the whole of civil society: chambers of commerce and voluntary groups; arts and academics; professional bodies in science, medicine, law, finance, and education; rural and urban life; faith groups, campaign groups, consumer groups, and conservation groups. Having had their places allocated, each group would be able to send their own chosen representatives appointed within a set of guidelines to ensure credibility and transparency. Political parties would not be excluded; their role in the life of the nation clearly merits recognition, and they would also provide a vital link to the Commons and experience of political decision making. Their numbers could be either directly elected or appointed by the parties themselves based on general election vote shares.

This simple step would secure the constitutional role of the House of Lords for generations to come. More importantly, it would bring community groups in their widest sense fully into the structures of power and decision making in the UK. It is hard to imagine a more potent declaration that the role of the community is being recognised as central to the future wellbeing of our nation.

So far we have looked at the community primarily as a network of relationships, ranging from the most intimate relationships within couples and families to the broader networks that define the level of social capital within an area or a nation. These relationships are formed by people, but they do not develop in isolation from their surroundings. The physical environment of bricks and mortar and the national and regional structures which shape our wider identity can have a profound effect on whether community is able to grow and flourish. Without these external environments, even getting the relational contexts right may not be sufficient to achieve the community renaissance that we so urgently need.

9

RE-SHAPE THE NATION

My country, right or wrong; if right, to be kept right; and if wrong, to be set right.

CARL SCHURZ

Patriotism is, fundamentally, a conviction that a particular country is the best in the world because you were born in it.

GEORGE BERNARD SHAW

Within a few weeks of my parents moving into their new home in a small Cambridgeshire village, we started discovering food on the doorstep. Generally it was fruit and veg, and as time went on we found that the mysterious deliveries tended to reflect what was growing well in that particular season. One year it was marrows; we ate so many of the things that it was a good 20 years before I could look another marrow in the face. Food wasn't the only thing that had a habit of turning up unannounced at the Anderson house. We rarely locked the back door during the day, and it was not unusual for friends and neighbours to just wander into the kitchen looking for my parents.

The village had a deep reservoir of community relationships, which brought both benefits and obligations. Social isolation was neither a risk nor an option. When one elderly lady was moving house and the amount of stuff she had accumulated proved too much for the removal men to pack and load in a single day, our family was memorably called upon to open a one-night-only bed and breakfast 'because there's nowhere else in the village for them to stay'. When we subsequently moved again to a London suburb, my mother considered it perfectly natural to organise a pancake tossing race down the middle of our street on Shrove Tuesday.[94] This was a normal part of village life, but was considered so unusual in south-west London that it actually made the local paper.

If these were just isolated examples they could be written off as bucolic stereotypes, but in fact they reflect a much wider pattern. Attractive country towns and villages are imagined as nice communities to live in. City suburbs are seen as pleasant enough but sometimes a bit cold and distant. And inner city housing estates are viewed as places where you fear your neighbours rather than getting to know them. Of course there are exceptions, with closed rural communities and vibrant inner city enclaves. But why is it that just by looking at a place, we make judgements about the type of community that will have formed within it, and very often those judgements will be near enough accurate?

The fact is, the physical layout and characteristics of a place do make a real difference to its ability to support thriving communities and develop social capital. Our 1950s former council estate was conventionally laid out, with houses fronting onto the roads and having generous front and rear gardens. Just a short distance away, the 1960s and 1970s estates which followed adopted a radical design involving pedestrian walkways, communal grassed areas, rear access roads with garage blocks, and generally smaller gardens. They are complex and counter-intuitive to navigate, which makes them intimidating for outsiders to enter. There are no natural thoroughfares, which means the footways feel deserted and unsafe, especially at night. The open spaces belong to no-one and become unkempt havens for antisocial behaviour. Children living in houses with tiny yards or in flats with no outdoor space at all spend much of their time indoors, because parents do not feel confident to allow them outside. And as we have already seen, areas like these with large concentrations of social housing suffer the double blow of being the hardest places to form community and being filled with people who, by virtue of their circumstances, find it most difficult to contribute.

Town centres too follow a 'pecking order' of desirability. At the top are traditional high streets of historic buildings populated with quirky independent stores. Below this comes the mainstream 'high street', its character largely stripped out by a proliferation of chain stores but still providing everyday shoppers with most of what they need. Struggling town centres gradually lose the clothing and higher-end retail stores, to be replaced with pound shops, takeaways, charity shops, and gambling outlets. At the bottom of the scale the shutters and graffiti start to take over. Large modern estates seem to have given up on the idea of the town centre altogether, relying almost entirely on the car to access out-of-town superstores and retail parks. This prevents the risk of urban decay but also precludes any possibility of developing a thriving local identity.

Location and employment patterns also work to define the character of a community. When Corringham grew to its current size it was an oil refinery town. Most people worked in one of a fairly small number of heavy industries along the Thames estuary. It would not be uncommon to share both a workplace and social activities with your immediate neighbours. Even the local pub was named The Catcracker, after the towering structure in the refinery that broke down crude oil into petrol. Today almost all of those industries (and the Catcracker pub itself) are gone. Those who are not already retired either take the train into London or drive to other more remote and diverse places of employment. Working days are longer as a result (it is quite normal for a London commuter to work a 12-hour day once travel times are added in), and people's relationships and social lives are no longer connected to a geographical area. Workmates could come from anywhere within a 100-mile, 10-million strong London catchment, and what happens in work, stays in work.

This 'dormitory town' arrangement seems almost calculated to inhibit community life. The town consists mostly of densely packed residential areas with relatively few amenities. It has no clear sense of identity, having developed through the post-war merging of two small villages. Despite having a population of 30,000 people it is neither a historic market town nor a local centre in the way that would define other towns of similar size. It has no surrounding hinterland to make it a natural focus, is not at the hub of a transport network, and no-one really comes into the town unless they already live there. Its two separate centres both lack critical mass, and while they are surviving commercially, one suffers from lack of scale and the other from poor-quality 1960s design which makes it a lively precinct by day but an uneasy no-mans-land after the shops close.

Despite all of these challenges, Stanford and Corringham is still in many ways an attractive place to live. It remains a safe and affordable area to buy a house and raise a family; something which sets it apart from much of the wider London area which intersperses zones of unattainable wealth with pockets of real social deprivation. It has decent state schools and reasonable employment prospects. Its council estates are the most challenging areas of the town, but still rank among the least-worst social housing in Thurrock. It lacks accessible green spaces, but even that may be changing with the opening of a new riverside country park on a reclaimed former landfill site nearby. It would seem to offer all of the basic conditions to promote wellbeing, but as we have seen, the evidence suggests otherwise. It is clear that almost all of the problems must be down to relational factors. The community does not quite function as it could and should, and it is possible to 'read' much of this in the physical environment itself without any knowledge of people's lives at all.

Planning gain

Traditionally it was said that a village had to have a church, a town a market, and a city a cathedral.[95] This reflected a centuries-old pattern of predominantly rural village life, with towns serving as local commercial centres, and cities providing regional administrative and cultural hubs. The size and layout of these settlements closely reflected the lifestyle of their communities, and it would be fair to describe their growth as, in many respects, 'community led'. It is perhaps no co-incidence that settlements which remain closest in size and scale to these historic roots are often those which are seen as the most attractive places to live and continue to show high levels of social capital.

Industrialisation and economic development in the eighteenth and nineteenth centuries brought significant and rapid change. New industries led to increased urbanisation and a mass migration of workers from more rural areas. Some towns and cities grew rapidly in size, while in other places entirely new communities sprang up. Both nineteenth-century pit villages in the northern coalfields and twentieth-century refinery towns on the Thames estuary are examples of this trend. If traditional settlements were shaped by communities, this was now very much market-led development. Initially houses for industrial workers were cheap, cramped, and densely packed. Urban slums became home to a new kind of poverty, and one of its characteristics was the absence of traditional community support structures which had developed over generations in more rural areas.

Already by the early twentieth century it was clear that towns and cities no longer provided an acceptable living environment for many of their inhabitants. Inner-city slums still existed despite the efforts of Victorian reformers, and a rising population was leading to urban sprawl. The situation came to a head after the Second World War, when widespread aerial bombing caused large scale destruction in many industrial cities. Nearly 4 million houses were destroyed, and it was obvious that the post-war reconstruction effort would need to involve building and re-building on a massive scale.

The 1947 planning act brought unprecedented levels of state control into the future of British settlements. For the first time, it became a legal requirement that any significant new development would require planning permission. In future, government officials would decide what could be built and where. Add to this a massive programme of publicly funded council house building, and the era of state-led development had arrived. When measured by the volume of homes built and the number of people re-housed, the post war reconstruction was a success. But it also led to a disastrous experimentation with modernist estates and tower blocks which, decades later, still remain a focus for crime and social breakdown.

The modern British planning system is characterised by an uneasy relationship between the state and market. Locations where development can take place are severely restricted, with 'green belts' set in place to prevent the growth of existing settlements and allocation of new land for building constrained by local plans. The net result is that the market price for building land, set by rising demand and seriously constrained supply, remains high. This leads to large windfall profits for landowners and developers when new permissions are granted, and pushes the market price of houses to levels which are unaffordable for most average wage-earners. It also leads to a paradox in public attitudes to development: people complain that house prices are too high, but they also consistently oppose new developments in their local area because they will have to live with the consequences while having no personal stake in the rewards and benefits (financial or otherwise).

It is clear that no single actor has the capacity to shape the physical development of functional communities alone. The state has the power to regulate but seems unable to balance the range of economic and social factors involved. If we are honest, most of the very 'worst' areas are those which bear the heaviest imprint of state planning. It has also proved vulnerable to policy fads which sound good in the corridors of power but consistently fail at street level. The market will deliver a product for a price, but becomes distorted by the fact that developers are able to reap the financial rewards without bearing any of the wider 'costs'. Simple market forces alone would lead to house builders concreting over well-known beauty spots, because the location would command a high price and the wider social cost (the loss of open space for everyone to enjoy) is borne by neither the buyer nor the seller. Only the community has the capacity to evaluate and balance these kinds of decisions. The benefits of more abundant (and therefore cheaper) local housing or a new industrial estate providing employment can be weighed in people's minds against the increased traffic, pressure on local facilities, and loss of open space that they will bring. They may bring positive benefits too (more families living in an area might prevent the closure of a village school or post office), and tradeoffs can be made ('this is worth doing if we get some road improvements and a new health centre'). What the community lacks is any mechanism for deploying this capacity in practice. It has neither the financial power of the market participants nor the formal control of the local planners. Attempts are made at 'consultation', but these are broad in nature and vulnerable to being dominated by special interest groups who have a particular interest in the outcome.

Let's imagine there are two options available for building a couple of hundred new homes in a particular area. One is a former industrial site near the town centre. The land is contaminated and will require extensive clean-up. It is constrained in size and will involve higher density townhouses and apartments. It is well served by transport links and there are schools and a clinic nearby, although not those with the best reputations. The second site is on open land at the edge of town. Existing houses in the area will lose their country views, and the need to drive to reach jobs and services means that the roads will become busier. The site could accommodate traditionally designed houses with gardens, which people would prefer to live in (and would command a higher price). These are just the main factors, and the more you look into the detail there are dozens of smaller points which would also influence the choice. How do you make the decision? The market will usually prefer to go for the green field site: it's cheaper to develop and easier to sell. The local plan will generally favour the urban brown field site; it regenerates the town centre and is more efficient in transport and environmental terms. This reflects a conflicted choice in the community itself. People do want nice houses in a pleasant setting that produces a real 'community feel', but they also want to redevelop a run-down part of town, protect open spaces, and avoid the roads becoming clogged with traffic.

At present the developers would apply for planning permission, and market forces dictate that they will offer as little as possible in return in order to maximise profits on the development. The planning system will test the proposal for a minimum standard of compliance against rules and policies, and may also demand contributions towards local infrastructure. Wider community issues are considered, but with only limited options available to do anything tangible about them.[96]

Basically we are asking the market the wrong question. Rather than 'how do I maximise profits from development', the real question should be 'how do I maximise the community benefits of development while still making a profit'? It is true that the principle benefits of development are intrinsic. People do need homes to live in, commercial buildings to work or grow a business in, and so on. But there are a whole range of other factors which are currently being overlooked or undervalued in the decision-making process. The market ought to be good at managing this type of complexity and coming up with innovative ideas and solutions, provided that a means can be established for putting a value on the indirect benefits and costs. The community has the means for assessing those values, and the state can provide a regulatory framework which forces them to be taken into account.

Our new system might take the form of a 'social value auction'. Developers would make their proposals based on the total social value which could be delivered. Features which encourage community wellbeing (good layout and design, community facilities, human scale) are scored positively, while those which tend to damage it (transport congestion, insular lifestyles, environmental degradation) count against. Planning professionals employed by the state would carry out the formal evaluations, not on the basis of compliance with a pre-defined local plan but by auditing and confirming the social value embodied in the scheme. The community is given a direct influence by setting the criteria and values by which the various features will be 'scored'. This should be done with reference to real proposals and real choices; markets are only able to determine the truth of people's opinions in the context of actual transactions. The proposal which offers the greatest social value will be the one that is given permission to proceed. At a local level this provides a practical method for developing strategic plans. A particular planning authority might decide that it intends to allow a certain number of homes or industrial units, and will prioritise locations using a social value auction at the plan development stage. If adopted nationally it could potentially remove the need for central planning altogether. A sufficiently robust and well accepted system for evaluating social value could allow any scheme which ranked positively overall to go ahead, regardless of preconceptions about zoning or master plans.

This mechanism may also give a framework for equitably resolving the NIMBY issue.[97] It is often the case that even something which brings clear community benefits to a wider area can impact negatively on those closest to it. Ask someone if they want a housing development next door and they will invariably answer 'no'. Ask if they would accept it if offered several thousand pounds in compensation and their answer may change. Social capital auctions could include these direct financial compensation elements where appropriate, paid either to individuals (which will certainly challenge their viewpoint) or in some cases collectively to a community (increased congestion is rarely confined to the immediate neighbours).

Providing a mechanism for local opposition and community benefit to be fairly and transparently weighed against each other should finally open the door to a resurgence of housebuilding in the UK. We saw earlier how a lack of new housing has helped to push house prices in Britain to the very edge of affordability for most people. Prices are determined by supply and demand, and reflexive opposition to any new developments has led to a situation of too much demand chasing not enough supply. Pitting the irresistible force of development profits against the immovable object of planning laws has proved a poor means of regulating the housing market. A new settlement based on freedom to build for those who can creatively generate (and prove) social value may at last help to unblock the log-jam, releasing jobs, prosperity, and homes which are 'affordable' not because they are rationed out by a social housing provider but because people can actually afford to buy them and live in them.

United states?

It's not just planning laws which shape communities. The two big issues of national identity facing post-referendum Britain are the nature of our future relationship with Europe after we leave the EU, and the future of the United Kingdom itself (will England, Scotland, Wales, and Northern Ireland now remain a single nation)? Both are frequently presented as economic arguments, phrased in terms of who would be 'better off' under one scenario or another. There are certainly economic consequences, but as we have already seen, even a 10% shift in national prosperity makes little difference to the happiness and wellbeing of a developed nation. The real question is: how will these decisions shape our relationships and identity, and therefore our wellbeing as individuals and communities?

Ever closer union

It is easy to forget that Britain's 'relationship with Europe' is precisely that – a relationship. One that has 40 years of history behind it (or over a thousand years if you take the long view), and does not come to an end simply because we have decided to leave the EU. As Britain negotiates the terms of our departure, questions about the future shape of that relationship are re-opened for the first time in a generation and the answers are by no means clear.

All relationships involve an element of give and take. Or put another way, they involve some level of surrender of sovereignty. In the sphere of personal relationships, we have already seen that the more individual sovereignty people choose to surrender (by increasing their level of commitment through marriage), the higher their average life satisfaction. And while you can't automatically read that statistic across into relationships between nations, the basic principle is unavoidable. Closeness of relationship brings its rewards, and relinquishing some sovereignty is the price of relational proximity.

The fundamental question which Britain now has to answer is 'how close a relationship do we want with other European nations?', and by implication 'how much independence of action are we willing to give up to achieve it?' The European single market is built on the idea of 'four freedoms': the free movement of goods, services, capital, and labour. Free movement of goods and services requires a willingness to accept shared rules on things like vehicle safety standards, selling of insurance products, or (apocryphally) the straightness of bananas. Free movement of capital imposes budgetary discipline on member states and drives adoption of the Euro as a shared currency. And free movement of workers prevents controls on migration and generally means that welfare benefits must be available to all. By a margin of more than two to one, 'Remain' voters felt that free movement of people was a price worth paying for free access to European markets. 'Leave' voters believed the exact opposite, and felt by a similar two to one margin that free movement of people must be ended even if that meant losing full single market access. Viewed in these terms, the meaning of the Brexit vote is clear. Britain now intends to assert greater control over who can live and work within our borders, and will accept a more distant trading relationship as the price to be paid.

While Britain has chosen to bring the matter to a head, the same questions of relationship and sovereignty apply within the EU itself. In the run-up to the UK referendum, Europe has continued to experience an ongoing financial crisis. The causes have been developing for a while, and at their root is the fact that different nations within Europe made a decision to share the same currency, interest rates, and exchange rates, without sharing the same financial and economic policies.[98] Monetary policies that suit a successful industrial economy like Germany are not the same as those which would benefit a less developed economy like Greece. The differences are probably no greater than those between states in America or between different regions of the UK, but in the USA and UK there is political union as well as monetary union.

This gives an ability to have taxation and spending policies which even out the economic differences between areas. Although both economies have their own problems, it would not be possible to have a Dollar crisis or Pound crisis of the same type as the recent Euro crisis.[99]

There are two possible long-term futures for Europe, and both depend more on national and cultural identity than on blind economics. One option is to return to the idea of sovereign nations joined together in an alliance of common interest, low trade barriers, and mutual security. This goes back to the founding structures in political terms (a combination of European NATO and the 'common market'). It will happen if concepts of cohesion within European nations are strong but those between nations are weak. The other option is to create a more federal Europe, with a European government that controls a significant degree of financial and economic policy as well as monetary policy. This would provide economic stability and international clout, but it depends on a sense of European identity and cohesion which is at least equal to the individual national versions. It would require a permanent willingness for Europeans to see themselves as 'one people', accepting the responsibility to support one another and share prosperity indefinitely, even if this means there will be 'winners and losers' compared to the current status quo.

This question continues to divide nations, communities, and political parties. For some, a 'united states of Europe' has been a barely concealed objective for a long time. They attract the reluctant support of those for whom the idea of Europe makes sense in the globalised world of the twenty-first century in a way that it did not in the twentieth. London, Paris, Athens, and Stockholm look very different when viewed from each other, but these differences are minor when seen from the perspective of Mumbai or Beijing. But for others it represents a destruction of national identity and an extension of unaccountable, inefficient bureaucracy and is to be fought against at all costs.

For Britain, the decision of 'in or out' has also often presented in economic terms, but the relational and cultural drivers have always been at least as important. Now that the decision to leave has been made, what would an assessment based on the effects of Brexit on our national wellbeing tell us about Britain's future relationship with Europe? The basic things we are seeking are (as always) physical security, financial sufficiency, and thriving relationships. From a security perspective, closer ties are better than more distant ones. Not only have Europeans up to the mid-twentieth century had a pretty dark history of warring amongst ourselves, the kind of threats we are likely to face in the twenty-first century no longer respect international borders and positively thrive on division. Terrorism, organised crime, cyber attacks, and hybrid warfare demand a co-ordinated and united response across the whole of the conflict space, not just the bits defined by national boundaries. Whatever name we give to the future political structures, close co-operation with our neighbours and allies is essential to our future security.

Britain is the most connected large economy in Europe. Around 60% of our gross domestic product is 'external' meaning that it depends on either imports or exports.[100] This means that we have more to gain than most countries from free and unrestricted trade, and more to lose from finding ourselves on the wrong side of trade barriers or outside of the bodies that make the rules. However, we have already seen that GDP alone is a poor indicator of our happiness and wellbeing. Attempts to calculate the exact amount that we stand to gain or lose from retaining access to the single market are not only based on wild guesses and assumptions; they are also pretty pointless. Our future wellbeing in truth does not depend on a few tens of billions added to or removed from our national income, no matter how mind-bogglingly large those numbers may seem. Britain already has enough to ensure that everyone can live above the point of material sufficiency, but still has much to do in order to convert this prosperity into wellbeing for all. The crucial question may turn out to be: 'Is the kind of radical innovation that will be needed compatible with the inertia of a rules-based international club designed around solving the problems of the last century?' If (for example) changes to ensure full employment are declared incompatible with current European rules of free movement, we are faced with a choice between accepting permanent unemployment for millions or leaving the single market altogether. This is not a choice that any nation should be forced to make, and it is on these issues of economic innovation that the debate should be focused, not marginal percentage shifts in economic output.

The same barriers to change and innovation must also be overcome in the area of relational wellbeing. European institutions remain attached to well-intentioned but faltering policies of the twentieth century such as multiculturalism, political correctness, indiscriminate tolerance, and rights over responsibilities. To move on from them requires us to make some bold choices, and if those choices turn out to be constrained by rules which the EU is unwilling or unable to change this again may be a key factor in determining our relationship. The future of Europe needs to be based on solidarity, reciprocity, and hospitality. Reciprocity provides the 'natural justice' that makes people see the relationship as a fair one, and decision making based on hospitality expressed at community level gives them back a sense of control. With these things in place, the focus can move away from fear of unmanaged immigration and back onto the shared culture and values that bind Europe together in meaningful solidarity.

United nation

The same basic factors also affect the future of the United Kingdom itself. Our own community of nations is a product of history, and the joins are still visible. British English is distinct from any other kind, but Scottish, Welsh, and Irish English (and the Welsh language)[101] are also linguistically distinct. Our laws, government, and national traditions are based on 'union' rather than 'uniformity'; even our national flag is a composite built up from the nations of the UK. Our tribal identities strongly reflect which part of the UK we come from. Importantly, the dividing lines for each component of sub-national identity fall in roughly the same place. We all know where the line between Scotland and England falls, even if it would be barely visible from Athens, let alone Beijing.

For decades, wealth in the UK has been redistributed from stronger economic areas (currently London and south-east England) to weaker ones (post-industrial areas of northern England, Wales, Scotland and Northern Ireland). This process has continued with only occasional grumbling from those who pay the taxes to fund it, and provides strong practical evidence that a 'community of solidarity' exists within the nation. British identity has been forged by history experienced together, institutions built together, and wars fought together. This sense of being one nation goes beyond economic arguments. We are one people, therefore to support others is to support our own.

The future of the UK depends on recognising the fact that Englishness, Welshness, Scottishness, Irishness and Britishness are all parts of our culture. The balance between them has always been dynamic and fluid, shifting over years and centuries. The structure of the UK has to reflect those changes. We should neither force ourselves apart nor together beyond the reality of our shared and separate components of cultural identity. The state and the market cannot impose these changes; ultimately the community is the foundation upon which both rest. But politics in particular has an important role to play, because while cultural solidarity and identity may be subtle and complex ideas, a referendum to split up the nation is very much an either/or decision.

The impact on wellbeing of breaking up the UK would follow a broadly similar analysis to that which drives the future of our relationship with the European Union. Imposing borders between friends and neighbours will come with a cost. Security would be harmed (more opportunity for criminals to hide and opponents to divide), and prosperity damaged (a single nation is the ultimate 'free trade area', and anything else is second-best when it comes to economic co-operation and mutual support). However, when you listen to the most passionate separatists, this is not really what seems to drive them. Rather like the anti-immigration lobby in the Brexit debate, they feel that their culture and identity is under threat and see isolationism as the only way to protect it. At the time of the Scottish independence referendum in 2014 the case for leaving looked to be roughly balanced in financial terms, with the economic damage for Scotland mostly mitigated by tax revenues from North Sea oil. When the international oil price subsequently collapsed in 2015 the sums no longer added up, but the calls for independence continued to become ever more strident despite losing both the democratic and economic arguments.

The most effective way to put Britain's intra-national relations back onto a sustainable footing which promotes wellbeing rather than anger and resentment is to create devolved power structures which accurately reflect both the solidarity and the distinctive regional identities that exist within the UK. At the moment the separatists have it too easy; they can stir up a sense of resentment against the wider nation by blaming every problem on decisions made in London or a failure to provide them with financial subsidies. This makes a great political soundbite but in the long run it is profoundly disempowering. It robs communities of control over their own future and replaces it with a seething sense of blame and entitlement. This is the council estate mentality written large, and it is pretty much guaranteed to erode virtually every aspect of happiness and wellbeing once it takes hold. It provides a shortcut to the sense of anger and grievance which we identified at the start of this book, and of course that suits the more angry and populist strand within nationalism down to the ground because they are the main beneficiaries at the ballot box.

Not all nationalists fall into this category, and the best way to combat the more cynical element is to call their bluff. Given that they are calling for greater independence, they can hardly complain if they are given a measure of it. Real devolution of power means giving control over both taxation and public spending, so that regional communities are empowered to make their own decisions and live with the consequences. The idea that the Scottish people would prefer to live in a higher taxed, higher spending, more all-encompassing state than the English has often been asserted but never actually tested in practice. Proper devolution will give the next generation of politicians and voters the chance to decide for themselves.

We have seen how the nature of the communities and nations in which we live can have a big impact on happiness and wellbeing, for good or bad. But the problem of markets failing to take into account the wider impact of their actions and states encouraging division rather than unity is not just confined to property developers and nationalist politicians. It affects many other areas too, and the largest and most pressing of these is the global environment. Polluting the land, sea and air can be an easy way to make a fast buck, but it falls to the rest of society and on generations not yet born to clean up the mess. Evaluating the social costs and benefits of local developments is difficult enough. Coming up with a practical method for doing so when faced with global environmental issues like deforestation and climate change seems almost impossible. But unless we do so we run a real risk of changing our environment for ever. Ultimately human wellbeing is not just supported by economic and social factors. It is sustained by the finite resources of the planet, which we hold in trust for ourselves and our children. And it is to the global challenges of stewarding these resources that we must finally turn.

10

SAVE THE WORLD

Our most basic common link is that we all inhabit this planet. We all breathe the same air. We all cherish our children's future. And we are all mortal.

JOHN F. KENNEDY

What is the use of a house if you haven't got a tolerable planet to put it on?

HENRY DAVID THOREAU

In 2005 I decided that I was going to save the planet by putting cooking oil in my car's fuel tank.

Diesel bought at the pumps is a fossil fuel, derived from oil. When burnt in a car's engine, it produces carbon dioxide which is a 'greenhouse gas' and one of the main contributors to global warming. In theory at least, it is possible to burn other forms of oil such as vegetable oils in the same type of engine with minimal modification. Because plants absorb carbon dioxide from the atmosphere as they grow, this cancels out the emissions produced when they are burnt and makes them a 'carbon neutral' fuel source.[102]

Over the next two years we ran the car almost continuously on our home made 'bio-diesel', saving maybe six tonnes of carbon dioxide emissions in the process. This sounds pretty good, until you compare it with the 100 million tons pumped out by domestic cars in the UK each year. But as far as I was concerned if everyone else 'did their bit' in the way that we were doing, together we could make a big change for the better.

I started to have doubts in late 2007, when the news began to report a global surge in food prices. The price of basic foodstuffs such as wheat, rice and maize doubled within six months, leading to riots and protests in many poor countries where food forms a major part of living costs. I could tell that it was true; the price of a litre of cooking oil to put in our car had also jumped by 50%. The reasons for the 2007 food price shock were complex and analysts still do not fully agree on the causes. There is no real evidence for crop failures or population growth as a root cause. Rising incomes and changing tastes in developing countries certainly made a contribution. It takes 7kg of grain to produce just 1kg of beef, and more of the world's emerging middles classes can now afford this option which was formerly restricted to a rich-world minority. Reduced strategic reserves and the growing power of financial markets may have meant that speculation exaggerated the effect. But one of the big contributors was almost certainly the rapid growth of bio-fuel production on a commercial scale, encouraged by US and European government subsidies. Many crops can be sold either as food or for bio-fuels depending on which is more profitable, and even dedicated fuel crops are competing for the same finite area of agricultural land. The world is capable of sufficient food production to feed every stomach, but if we also add in the burden of filling every petrol tank there will simply not be enough productive land to go round. Given the difference in global incomes, the most likely result of a full-scale switch is that European and American drivers boast about their environmental credentials while African and Asian children suffer from malnutrition.

My simple environmental campaign was starting to look a whole lot more complex. I had started down the line of bio-fuels in part because climate change hits the world's poor hardest, but now it seemed that my actions were protecting their environment at the cost of feeding their families. Within a year the big old diesel was sold, and replaced with a more efficient car that could travel nearly twice the distance on a litre of fuel (now bought from a petrol station).

Out of sight, out of mind

Throughout that period, I was making deliberate efforts to act as an informed and environmentally aware citizen. Classic market theory suggests that most producers and consumers are less scrupulous. The average driver may be aware of the environmental impact of car use, but it does not affect their decision to fill up the tank. Neither they nor the petrol company have to pay anything at the pumps to compensate for the carbon dioxide that their car will emit as a result. The 'costs', which may take the form of anything from rising sea levels and arctic melting to environmental degradation and extreme weather events, are borne by global society and by future generations. This in turn means that people are more likely to buy and use petrol and diesel (and therefore to spend money going out exploring and drilling for the stuff). If you can have all the benefits of driving without paying for the full environmental cost of your actions, that makes the purchase more economically attractive.

Economists call these hidden costs *externalities*. They get their name from the fact that they are external, or separate, to the basic buying and selling that is going on in the market. My total cost of motoring includes the purchase price of the car, tax and insurance, maintenance and the fuel I put in it to make it go. In addition to the environmental damage, there are other externalities too which I never pay for at all. My car contributes to congestion which makes everyone late for work. That comes at a cost (they may lose wages, go off sick through stress, or get fired), but it is paid by them not me. The health service will pick up the tab for treating any injuries from accidents I am involved in, the local council repair the roads, and the police cover the cost of dealing with dangerous driving and car crime. I pay for all of this through my taxes, but so do other taxpayers, even those who neither own nor use a car.[103]

One of the oldest and simplest manifestations of externalities is the so-called 'tragedy of the commons'. It gets its name from the traditional practice of having common land in local communities, on which anyone had a right to graze their animals. Where there is plenty of land and cultural or practical limits on how many animals anyone can own, the idea of a commons is simple and works well. However, there is always the temptation for a farmer to put just a few extra sheep on there. He will profit as a result, and others will soon join him in increasing their number of animals too. The result will be over-grazing, and the number of sheep that the land can support will start to fall. We now have a crisis on our hands. Animals will die and everyone suffers as a result. In the end, the entire community is worse off than when they started, with a degraded natural asset and less overall capacity to earn their livelihoods and support themselves.

Once you understand the principle, you start to see examples of the commons everywhere. The cod population in the North Sea has collapsed by 75% since the 1970s because of overfishing. It would have been possible to reduce fishing to sustainable levels, but there was no practical incentive for fishermen to do so. If one boat voluntarily stayed in port that didn't preserve the stocks, it just meant that someone else got them instead. National quota systems have failed to restore the cod population, because everyone is still incentivised to bend or break the rules (or demand unrealistic quotas) before someone else does. Tropical forests are cut down and burnt to make way for plantation crops, which remain viable for just a few years before the soil degrades and the chainsaws move on. Even man-made resources like roads could be seen as a commons. If we all changed our driving habits then congestion could be avoided. But because not driving doesn't benefit me personally, it just makes the road a bit clearer for someone else, no-one does it.[104]

We are starting to realise that the entire global environment behaves like an enormous commons. One of the consequences of industrialisation and development has been that vast quantities of pollutants have been emitted, whether industrial effluents, domestic waste, or carbon dioxide from burning fossil fuels. It is increasingly clear that current levels of environmental emissions will cause damaging changes on a global scale, something which will make the decline of the North Sea fish stocks look minor by comparison.

Stop in the name of the law

The simplest responses to environmental damage have been laws which controlled or banned a particular practice. When I worked at West Thurrock power station, considerable amounts of equipment were installed purely to reduce our environmental impact. In between the boilers and the chimneys we had electrostatic precipitators, which captured fine dust and ash and stopped it going out into the atmosphere. As well as coating everything with an unpleasant grey film, these fine particles can cause smog and breathing problems. The chimneys themselves had optical sensors installed to check that we were not producing black soot, another source of air pollution and a probable carcinogen. The coal burners had been specially redesigned to reduce nitrogen oxides (NOx), one of the main causes of acid rain.

These types of environmental laws work best when there is a technical or practical solution which can mitigate the damage, and the benefits of doing so clearly outweigh the costs. They have the advantage that this cost-benefit calculation can include the value of externalities, something which the market alone fails to take into account. Neither West Thurrock nor its electricity customers gained any direct benefit from fitting low NOx burners. The effects were actually felt hundreds of miles away in the forests of northern Europe. But by making it a legal requirement, West Thurrock was (entirely reasonably) prevented from saving money at the cost of damaging someone else's environment.

There were, however, two other important pollutants which continued to go straight up the chimney. These were carbon dioxide (the main greenhouse gas) and sulphur oxides or SOx (another potent cause of acid rain and asthma). Flue gas desulphurisation was then in its infancy, and would have been so expensive to install as a retro-fit that the plant could never have borne the cost. Carbon capture and storage (CCS) is still at the development stage even today, and questions remain over its long-term effectiveness and economic viability.

Governments can ban or set limits on power station emissions and a whole host of other pollutants, provided that the technology exists and it is viable to use it. These laws are pragmatic in nature, and basically require people to use the best practices available rather than indulging in a 'race to the bottom' to try and save costs. The smoke-belching, river-polluting 'dark satanic mills' of Victorian Britain or Soviet Russia have become obsolete and unnecessary. Environmental expectations have risen with improving technology, and it would be socially unacceptable to pollute now in a way that was common even half a century ago.

Where environmental legislation struggles is to deal with challenges that are widespread and cumulative in nature. Even if everyone drove the latest in fuel-efficient cars which met the strictest environmental standards, collectively we would still be emitting too much carbon dioxide. You can't prevent deforestation by requiring the loggers to put unleaded petrol in their chainsaws. Clean air rules for a city or region can and do work; London's 'great smog' of 1952 caused an estimated 12,000 premature deaths and led to the 1956 Clean Air Act which was credited directly with preventing a recurrence. But no-one has yet managed to come up with a similar set of enforceable rules which could halt climate change on a global scale.

The common good

If left to market forces alone, classic economic theory suggests that all attempts at holding resources 'in common' are doomed to over-exploitation and failure. The economists are probably being a little too pessimistic. A few miles from us at West Tilbury we have one of Britain's last remaining traditional areas of common land. Like most people, I would be completely unaware of its existence were it not for the fact that, as local councillors, we annually appointed one representative to a body known as the

'West Tilbury Common Conservators'. The common land itself dates back to medieval times, and it was on this very spot in 1588 that Elizabeth I gave her stirring speech on the eve of the Spanish Armada. By the eighteenth century a classic 'tragedy of the commons' was unfolding, with grazing rights being abused, increasing numbers of animals on the land, and a general degradation of the fields well underway. Rather belatedly, in 1895, the Conservators were established by Act of Parliament to monitor and enforce grazing rights and ensure the viability of the common for future generations. It worked. Even today, horses belonging to local families can be seen roaming free on the low-lying fields in the shadow of Tilbury power station.

It seems that West Tilbury is not alone in finding community-based solutions which survive the test of time. In 2009, economist Elinor Ostrom was awarded the Nobel Prize for her work, which identified the characteristics of successful community solutions to common pool resource management around the world. Ostrom concluded that a community can manage a commons successfully, provided that it has certain basic features in place. These include: clearly recognised boundaries; workable rules for resource allocation; participative community decision making; effective dispute resolution, monitoring and enforcement; and recognition by higher authorities. The West Tilbury Common Conservators meet all of these conditions. The boundaries are well established, they have clear byelaws to control use of the common, they are appointed by the local community, their decisions are enforceable, and they are legally recognised by Parliament.

Where Ostrom's conditions are met, community management is a real and attractive possibility. It has been shown to work for inshore fisheries, forests, grazing lands and irrigation water supplies. By empowering a community to solve its own environmental and economic problems, it both ensures material wellbeing and actively promotes relational wellbeing. Once the community is forced to get together to manage its common resources, it is then likely to work together in other ways too.

To have and to hold

Not every shared resource meets Elinor Ostrom's conditions for community management. Deep-sea fish will swim freely across borders, pursued by boats from many different communities. Even where some form of international agreement is possible, the lack of clear boundaries and involvement of multiple communities means that a 'Deep-Sea Fishery Conservators' is unlikely to work.

Before looking to anything more complex, it is worth asking the question 'why do we need common resources at all?' After all, the vast majority of fields around West Tilbury do not form part of the common. They are owned by individual farmers, who simply get on and grow crops on their own land. Fields can be bought and sold, passed on to the next generation, and so on. One of the big advantages of private property is that it allows the owners to make long-term commitments to improving it. Investments in fences, barns, soil condition, drainage and irrigation systems can take years to pay back. They bring benefits both to the farmer and to wider society (in the form of greater productivity and cheaper food to feed a growing population), but they are simply not possible without the security that private ownership of farmland brings. The majority of things which affect our lives (the fields in which our food is grown, the factories that supply our goods, and the houses we live in) are founded on property rights. The biggest recent experiment into collective ownership of assets was twentieth-century communism, and it was generally disastrous. Without any personal interest in the future of their farm, factory, or flat, people neglected the long term and just lived for the moment. The result was dilapidation and decay on a massive scale. It is probably no co-incidence that Thurrock's council estates (where most people do not own the properties they live in) are amongst its most deprived and run down areas.

The idea of private property rights seems to be a universal one. It is understood in almost every culture, even those which also practise forms of communal ownership. Societies where property rights are backed up by fair and enforceable laws show consistently higher levels of prosperity and wellbeing.[105] People are unlikely to commit to any form of long-term endeavour if corrupt officials could come and take it all away from them tomorrow. This is all fairly simple and obvious for things like businesses and factories and even farmland, but can it be applied to more complex and interdependent natural resources like fish stocks?

In 1976 after a series of international disputes known as the 'cod wars', Iceland finally secured exclusive fishing rights in a 200 mile radius around its shores. Straight away, they realised that simply excluding foreign boats was not going to solve all their problems. Icelandic fishermen were still catching 350,000 tonnes per year of cod, while scientists estimated that the sustainable limit was nearer 230,000 tonnes.[106]

The initial response of the government was to try to act as 'commons conservator', by limiting the number of days that fishing boats could put to sea. However, rather than reducing the amount of fish caught, this simply triggered an 'arms race' between different fishing companies and communities. Larger, faster and better equipped (but more expensive) boats could catch more fish in the limited time available. Communities located further from the fishing grounds suffered, as their transit times to fish were longer. In some cases even lives were put at risk, as boats put to sea in atrocious weather to make maximum use of the limited fishing season. The government response was to reduce the number of fishing days further, but to no avail. The catch remained at 300,000 to 400,000 tonnes, while estimated sustainable levels declined to below 200,000 tonnes. Fishermen struggled to pay for ever larger and more complex boats, knowing that if they did not win the dash to grab the fish first then someone else would.

By the 1980s it was obvious that time limits had failed. What the government did instead was to gradually introduce a system of individual transferable catch quotas. A total allowable catch was calculated for the year, and each fisherman was allocated a share of that catch. These shares behaved much more like private property. They could be bought and sold, transferred between boats or communities and so on. The effect was almost immediate. The total catch was brought down to sustainable levels and fish stocks started to recover. Fishermen could now spread their effort throughout the year using less fuel and expensive technology, meaning that their costs went down. More importantly, they became stakeholders in the long-term viability of the environmental resource. Rather than being incentivised to grab the biggest possible share of a declining pie, they saw that the value of their quota would increase if fish stocks recovered and grew (they would now own an equal share of a larger overall pie). Total catches actually declined through the early 1990s, the fish bounced back, and catches have remained stable in the region 200,000 to 250,000 tonnes ever since. Compare that to the North Sea area with its collapsing fish population, and it is clear that allocating property rights and using market mechanisms to conserve natural resources can have a real and valuable role to play.

Every breath you take

The bigger the shared resource, the more difficult it becomes to manage it fairly, sustainably and effectively. As Elinor Ostrom showed, individual communities can steward resources within their own direct control reasonably well. Iceland has proved that multiple communities can use the power of markets and property rights to assist them in handling the complexity of larger scale shared resources. And simple government legislation limiting harmful practices like avoidable power station emissions has a role to play. But we are increasingly realising that the entire global environment also behaves like a giant common resource, which we have no choice but to manage.

If we do not greatly reduce the amount of carbon dioxide produced by burning fossil fuels, future generations are likely to experience rising sea levels, loss of inhabitable and productive land, large-scale displacements of populations in low lying areas, permanent changes to rainfall and drought patterns, and an increase in extreme weather events.[107] The planet has a complex and interdependent 'carbon cycle', with land, sea, air and biomass all playing a part in regulating the climate. Like the West Tilbury common or the Icelandic fisheries, this system has a finite capacity to support human activity.

All of these changes will damage wellbeing. They will affect security and stability, harm prosperity, increase poverty and disrupt communities. However, to prevent them means burning less fossil fuels and thus slowing the rate of industrial and economic development. This harms wellbeing too, especially in the poorest developing nations. We would be shutting down the engine which has lifted over a billion people out of real material poverty in the last two decades alone. This creates a significant fairness issue: developing nations ask how it can be right that the path which others took to end poverty through economic development based on cheap fossil fuels can now be closed off to them? And it also suffers from the problem that the situation may not reach crisis point until decades or even a century into the future. That's not long in terms of human history, but it is easily long enough to produce behaviours rather like the 1970s Icelandic fisherman. If the end of the season is approaching, you might as well rush to grab your share before someone else does.

As we have seen, the reason that people carry on polluting is that they can do so without facing up to the full environmental cost of their actions (the externalities). If they bore these costs in full, they would probably find other ways of doing things. They would either invest in new and cleaner technology, or the market for their product would simply decline as people moved to other, less polluting alternatives. Fossil fuels would increasingly be used only for things where there were no practical alternatives, and in much smaller quantities than today.

Although unregulated 'free' markets cannot respond to the cost of externalities, it is entirely possible for the state to intervene and put a price on them. The market will then carry on making decisions, producing innovation and managing complexity, but now working to a different set of ground rules. So long as the price imposed on negative externalities like pollution fully covers the global impact of the likely environmental damage, then the market will naturally steer society away from such a costly course of action.

Two different methods of externality pricing have already been identified, and increasingly shown to work in practice.

The first is to impose a tax on any activity which generates negative externalities. In the case of carbon dioxide emissions leading to global warming, this would take the form of a 'carbon tax'. Estimates of the total global social and environmental damage from emitting each additional tonne of carbon dioxide vary significantly, but they are perhaps in the region of £100 per tonne (and the research is getting better all the time). This pretty much all comes from fossil fuels, so the tax can simply be imposed on fossil fuels burnt based on their carbon emitting potential.[108] To give an idea of what this would mean in practice, a £100 per tonne carbon tax would add about 25p to a litre of petrol, or £500 to the average annual household energy bill. In fact any activity which involves using fossil fuels directly or indirectly (driving a car, heating a home, or using energy intensive materials like steel and aluminium) would become more expensive, and market forces would encourage people to seek less polluting alternatives. So for example it would become more economically attractive to take the train, insulate your house, or replace structural aluminium with timber.

There are three main criticisms of such a tax. The first is that it imposes a burden on economic activity and growth, which itself has a negative impact on society. The simplest way to address this is to feed the money back into the economy by reducing other areas of taxation. So if the money from the carbon tax was used to reduce corporate and personal taxes, the net effect on businesses and households would be neutral. More polluting industries and lifestyles would still be penalised, but that is the whole point – our aim is to change behaviours by offering economic incentives to do so. Britain currently emits around 500 million tonnes of carbon dioxide per year. If this were taxed at £100 per tonne, the resulting £50 billion in tax revenues would allow income and corporation taxes to be reduced by more than a third.[109] The price of anything dependent on energy from fossil fuels would rise significantly, most obviously fuel and electricity prices, but also anything involving energy-intensive manufacture and transport. On average, no-one would be better off, but they would have more money in their pockets and more choice on how to spend it. And crucially, the most attractive choices would be those which did not involve creating costly carbon emissions.

The second argument is that unless everyone adopts the same system, any country that imposes a carbon tax disadvantages itself in international trade and simply moves the emissions problem somewhere else. Energy-intensive industries in Britain such as aluminium smelters would just shut down and relocate to a country with a more favourable tax regime. Until the 2016 referendum vote, the only feasible way to solve this problem seemed to be to persuade at least Europe, the USA and China to agree to a common approach. The international climate agreements signed in Kyoto (1997) and Paris (2015) took tentative steps in this direction, but on nowhere near the scale required. Having made the decision to leave the EU, Britain will now have to re-negotiate around 150 international trade agreements in which it previously participated via EU membership. This provides a unique window of opportunity to unilaterally adopt a carbon tax and to impose tariffs on energy-intensive manufactured goods originating from countries which do not have a similar system of their own, thus levelling the playing field for UK manufacturers compared to their international competitors. The challenges of doing so remain very significant, but one consequence of the Brexit vote is that the UK is now in a position to take genuine global leadership on climate change if we chose to do so.

The third argument is that the environmental costs of global warming are not evenly spread. Low lying areas or those affected by changing weather patterns will experience a disproportionate impact. At a national level, countries which are not likely to be badly hit may find it worthwhile to carry on emitting and allow their global neighbours to bear the pain. The obvious answer is to use at least some of the carbon tax revenues for climate change mitigation in the worst affected areas, but reaching international agreement on large-scale payments between nations is going to be harder even than setting up the carbon tax in the first place. A better solution is probably to set the carbon tax high enough that it is guaranteed to work. If the damaging effects of climate change are prevented, then how to compensate the victims becomes an academic question.

Finally it is worth noting that a carbon tax is not the only market-modification which is capable of setting a price for externalities. The other approach which has been tried is known as cap-and-trade and, rather than setting a direct price on the externality costs of climate change, it works by fixing a limit on the total emissions allowable. The first large scale cap-and-trade scheme was created by the European Union from 2005 onwards. The scheme applies to large energy intensive users and producers (about half of total emissions), but not small businesses or households. It sets a limit of around 2 billion tonnes across the 30 participating countries, with an intention that this will gradually reduce over time.[110] The scheme is based on tradable permits to emit carbon dioxide, rather like the Icelandic fishing quotas. Factories and power stations which emit more CO_2 have to buy extra permits, while those which manage to reduce their emissions can sell their surplus permits to others. As the 'cap' is reduced the laws of supply and demand should dictate that permits become more expensive, encouraging a switch to less polluting ways of generating and using energy. Market prices for carbon permits have swung between zero and €30 per tonne as the supply and demand position has varied, complicated by a global recession which reduced demand for almost everything and hence the energy required to manufacture and transport it. The market is estimating that prices may regularly reach €30 by 2020, and like all market predictions this is 'true' in the sense that you can buy a carbon futures option today to secure your position.

All of the same arguments about carbon taxes also apply to cap-and-trade schemes. Cap-and-trade is actually growing globally, with a UN system in place and systems for offsetting emissions and supporting developing countries being added on. In theory it offers more certainty about actual emission levels that will be achieved, as these are set by the chosen 'cap'. It still relies on research and government action to set the correct cap, just as a carbon tax depends on setting the right price. In the end, the decision on which one to adopt will be mostly a matter of practicality and politics. The carbon tax is more visible, with big changes in personal taxation and the prices of goods and energy reaching individual consumers. Cap-and-trade works more behind the scenes, with only gradually rising output costs in some areas being apparent. It is likely that as demands for environmental action grow big visible changes will become politically expedient, but until then anything that hides the costs will remain less politically risky.

11

COME THE GLORIOUS DAY

Action may not always bring happiness; but there is no happiness
without action.

BENJAMIN DISRAELI

Show me your faith without deeds, and I will show you my faith
by my deeds.

THE BIBLE

Stanford-le-Hope railway station has stood since 1854, when
it was at the end of the steam railway line built to serve the
new deep-water docks at Tilbury. Today the station has a
slightly down-at-heel feel, its small Victorian platform buildings
having long since been replaced by a functional but drab modern
ticket office. A million passengers per year use the station, with
the majority being London commuters who flood through every
morning and evening.

The more pessimistic 'Remain' campaigners predict difficult
times ahead for places like Thurrock. Its main employers are
logistics (driven by international trade) and financial services
in the City of London (which has flourished as Europe's leading
financial market). Both of these could be badly hit in the aftermath
of Brexit. With unemployment up and living standards down, they
would predict that Thurrock is likely to consolidate its place at the
bottom of the life-satisfaction league table. With this will come a
further increase in alienation, disaffection, and anger. Thurrock led
the way for Britain to exit the EU with one of the highest 'Leave'

votes in the country. Once it becomes clear that this has not led to the improvements in security, prosperity, and relationships that people desired, who knows what the next political movement to take root here could look like?

But it doesn't have to be that way. Imagine for a moment that in the crucial few years following the EU referendum, Britain chose to embrace a radical and positive vision for the future which had been so sadly absent during the referendum campaign itself. As a nation we used the opportunity offered by this once-in-a-generation shift in the political landscape to end unemployment, dismantle the social housing and benefits traps, reform the monetary system, promote a renaissance of community life, restore a generous confidence in our national identity, build truly liveable communities, and take global leadership to safeguard the environment for future generations. What would Britain ten tears after Brexit look like? Or if that is too big and abstract a question to answer, what would Thurrock look like?

At Stanford-le-Hope railway station, passenger numbers are up by 20%, after the effective elimination of unemployment led to the creation of 300,000 new jobs in the greater London area alone. As state funding was switched from paying out welfare benefits to encouraging companies to create jobs, everyone from shops to hospitals to factories to banks started taking on more staff. Entire categories of work which had virtually disappeared from the economy such as support staff, office assistants and junior training roles began to re-appear in the workplace. The new jobs were all at the lower paid end of the scale, but by providing a means for people to 'get a foot on the ladder' of employment and develop their skills and experience, many of the people who took them were soon able to move up.

As a relatively inexpensive area in easy reach of London, Thurrock has benefited disproportionately from all of this new employment. Peak hour trains have been extended from eight carriages to 12 in order to cope with the additional commuters but, in spite of this, the queues at the ticket windows which used to prove such a regular frustration are now fading into memory. The station took on extra staff once it became possible to offer them jobs without passing the cost on to the travelling public, including local young people who might previously have drifted from education into unemployment. Capital funding was made available using 'base load money' to extend London's cashless ticketing systems out into Essex. The platforms and station forecourt have a different feel too. For one thing they are larger; a new public transport interchange stands proudly in front of the redeveloped station concourse, and a smart café welcomes travellers with the chance to grab their morning caffeine fix. Everything is clean, tidy and well maintained, as there are now enough staff with time available to take a real pride in their workplace. Floral displays provide a more welcoming feel, and graffiti is a thing of the past.

There have been no reported crimes in the station car park for over six months. No-one is quite sure why; regular staff patrols and CCTV that actually gets monitored must be part of the answer, and the smart visual appearance of the area seems actively to discourage trouble. Crime right across the town is down as more of those who might previously have got involved in casual theft and vandalism are now out earning an honest living.

Walking up the hill towards the parish church, the area around the war memorial has a buzzing, continental feel. The entire area has been re-laid as a town square used by both pedestrians and vehicles. New cafés have extended out onto the pavement and are taking advantage of the good weather to do a steady trade. Catering has been one of the big winners in the new high-employment economy; lower staff costs have enabled enterprising local business owners to both improve service and reduce prices, meaning that trade is up and there is a real sense of community around the square.

Beyond the freshly planted spring flowers surrounding the war memorial itself, the old bank which stood boarded up for many years has now re-opened as an estate and letting agent. A screen in the window is playing an advertising graphic explaining how the new 14-year interest-free mortgage can enable you to own your own home in Stanford before your children leave school.

Prices have remained stable for the last ten years which has made speculation on property rather less attractive, but the big difference is that properties on what used to be known as the council estates are now on offer in the agent's window to rent or to buy. Somehow it is impossible to completely hide their 1970s social housing ancestry, but the proliferation of smart new windows and doors, well-tended gardens, and modern extensions is making it more and more difficult to tell them apart from their private market cousins.

Walking across the square your attention is brought back to reality by the horn of an electric white van. They have been getting more common since the introduction of the carbon tax, and there are now two charging points on the plaza. They are so quiet that you sometimes don't hear them coming, but at least the customers in the pavement cafés are spared the noise and diesel fumes. You could hail one of the electric taxis which are also starting to appear, but on a day like this you might as well grab an electric bike. To sweeten the pill of higher fuel prices the government has been putting some of the revenue back into local transport, and Thurrock is one of a number of areas which now benefits from the greatly expanded London cycle hire scheme.

Cycling along Stanford High Street you see that a number of new businesses have opened up. The retail economy has grown since the new rules increased employment and made investment easier, and towns like Stanford-le-Hope have been one of the winners. The additional trade has helped to finance urban regeneration, and one side of the high street now boasts a new shopping arcade with commercial units above. Lower staff costs have made local shops more viable, while increasing fuel and travel costs resulting from the carbon tax have helped to reduce the advantages of big out-of-town retail parks. Lakeside shopping centre is still a successful regional hub, but it has diversified into leisure activities and it does feel like Thurrock's traditional high streets are at last beginning a slow renaissance.

Continuing along the road towards Corringham, you turn right onto the tree-lined boulevard running through the heart of the old council estate. In theory cars are allowed along here too, but most don't bother to run the gauntlet of bikes, buggies, benches, and bollards which have claimed the new avenue. This was a much bigger project, and has taken the whole of the last ten years to come to fruition. Some houses and flats had to be demolished altogether to make it possible, although the number of properties on the estate has increased overall as new homes were built to close off the dingy alleyways that used to blight the area, especially at night. Most people no longer think of this as a council estate; all of the properties are available to rent or buy and a growing number of them are now owned by former tenants through the no-interest mortgage scheme. But behind the scenes, the regeneration could not have happened without the involvement of the local council. They still owned most of the land and many of the properties, and with all of this as collateral they were able to borrow the eight-figure sum needed to kick start the project in the form of an interest-free national loan. The rest of the investment came from a property developer; part of the social value bid which won them the right to develop a green field site on the edge of town was a commitment to help fund the estate redevelopment. They seem to have done OK out of it, as the new family homes they constructed on the estate at an expected loss turned out to be worth more than anyone initially thought. The award-winning redevelopment is now seen as a model for even more ambitious regeneration schemes taking place on former council estates up and down the country.

Emerging off the boulevard you enter Corringham Park, where you dock the bike and carry on up the re-laid footpath. At the top of the park is the stunning new permanent Youth Pavilion built and run by a local charity. The organisation is popular in the community and locals will tell you that they would have got there in the end anyway, but 100% match funding of donations through the government's community charity initiative certainly helped to speed things along. Not far from the new centre, the park warden is starting her rounds. The council transferred management of Thurrock's parks to community groups a few years ago, and taking advantage of the new simplified system for paying expenses and a retainer to volunteers the park is now immaculately maintained by a rota of semi-voluntary local wardens. In the community meeting room, a retired linguist is using her professional skills to help a small group of Arab women improve their English. Thurrock continues to become slowly more diverse, although not in the way that past critics would have feared. Around half of the newcomers are skilled professionals, mostly working in international shipping and connected with the new port. Those who came fleeing from chaos in the Middle East are here by the invitation of a local refugee support group, already in work, and increasingly well integrated into community life.

A final short walk brings you through into Corringham town centre, where the bus will pick you up to take you back to the station. Business is doing well here too, although nothing can disguise the poor 1960s design of the precinct. Eventually someone will come up with a solution. Rumour has it that a developer is buying up leases on flats and shops with a view to a regeneration scheme based on enhancing social value. Not everything has a simple or straightforward answer, but the success of other schemes around the country is starting to give people hope that here too, solutions will be found.

Most subtly but profoundly of all, the atmosphere has changed. The infamous 'Thurrock shrug' of resignation is seen less often around our town. Some of the spirit that once challenged medieval tyranny, repelled the Armada, and built the great industrial complexes of the nineteenth and twentieth centuries is starting to re-emerge. A decade ago no-one was surprised that Thurrock found itself propping up the league table of national wellbeing. Now the area is hovering somewhere around average, which in the circumstances feels like the greatest achievement of all.

And if all that doesn't cheer my neighbours up, I'm really not sure what will.

ACKNOWLEDGEMENTS

Thanks are due to all those individuals who encouraged, supported, or inspired me on my initial journey into politics, including Dr David Landrum, Jim Wallis, Elizabeth (now Baroness) Berridge, Andy Flannagan, Zoe Dixon, Colin Bloom, Alistair Burt MP and Andrew Selous MP.

I am grateful for the trust placed in me by the people of Stanford-le-Hope and Corringham who elected me as their local councillor, and by friends and colleagues in the Thurrock and South Basildon & East Thurrock Conservative Associations who voted for me as their group leader. Without the opportunity to serve you and to serve alongside you in local politics, all of this would just be empty theory. I also acknowledge the support of our two local Members of Parliament, Stephen Metcalfe MP and Jackie Doyle-Price MP, both of whom provide a welcome antidote to the stereotypes of politicians often portrayed in the media.

There are very few genuinely new ideas in this book. My privilege has been to tap into the rich vein of political thinking which remains a feature of the UK political scene and hopefully shape some of it into a practical form that is accessible to a wider audience. In this regard I am indebted to the work of four political think-tanks in particular: the Centre for Social Justice, the Jubilee Centre, Theos and ResPublica.

Two seminal reports helped clear the way for me to reconcile the challenge of engaging in secular politics as a Christian: 'Doing God' (Nick Spencer) and 'Talking God' (Jonathan Chaplin), both published by Theos. I must also acknowledge the prayerful encouragement of many friends in Thurrock Christian Fellowship and 24-7 Prayer, without whose support I would never have taken the plunge into political life.

Pete Greig had the gift and grace to help teach me how to write, Ian Nicholson and Justin Blake have supported me on the journey, and Stephanie Heald offered her experience and honesty to steer my initial ideas into something that may yet prove worth reading.

Finally I must pay tribute to the patience, kindness, and faith of my wife and family in supporting me as I have given time that could, and maybe should, have been theirs to politics and to writing. The casual way in which society treats politics as a blood sport and politicians as fair game shows scant regard for the effect on families and children. Lisa and the girls have accepted this with great courage and grace and I owe them a huge debt as a result.

ABOUT THE AUTHOR

Phil Anderson is a battle-hardened local politician based in Thurrock in South Essex, known to the national media as 'Britain's most Eurosceptic area' and 'the country's capital of misery' after it was identified as the worst borough in Britain for life satisfaction.

Phil won his council seat in Thurrock in 2010 by a nail-biting 29 votes. In 2011 he was elected as Conservative party leader and leader of the opposition in one of the highest profile marginal constituencies in the country, against a Labour majority of just one seat. After failing to retain the ward in 2014, Phil became the local Conservative party Chairman in advance of the 2015 general election, where Thurrock emerged as UKIP's top target in the UK. The Conservatives held the seat in what came to be seen as the definitive three-way marginal battleground and one of the key political bellwethers of the election.

Phil studied Engineering at Bristol University and his professional background is as a Chartered Engineer, project manager, and consultant. His previous political background is in community activism and issues-based campaigning, motivated primarily by his Christian faith and involvement in local church.

Prior to being elected, a spell as a consultant in the Foreign Office led Phil to working in the House of Commons, running events and an award-winning democratic engagement project. Working in close proximity with MPs and Peers was his catalyst for becoming involved in party politics, and he joined the Conservative party in 2009 and stood as a local councillor in 2010.

He has been a Director of the Thames Gateway Development Corporation and the Thurrock Racial Unity Support Taskgroup, and a regular media contributor in print, radio, internet and occasional TV.

Phil is married to Lisa and has two teenage daughters. In his limited spare time after work and politics he is a qualified private pilot and also enjoys running, cycling, and writing. He remains an active part of the local Christian community in Thurrock.

ENDNOTES

1 First ONS Annual Experimental Subjective Well-being Results, Office for National Statistics, 24 July 2012.
2 The ONS data provided four measures of subjective wellbeing. Thurrock was the lowest top-tier local authority area in the UK for 'mean average life satisfaction', which is the simplest way to produce an overall ranking table.
3 'A Short Guide to Gross National Happiness Index', The Centre for Bhutan Studies, 2012.
4 Robert F. Kennedy, Address to University of Kansas, Lawrence, Kansas, 18 March 1968, quoted on www.mccombs.utexas.edu. The full quote reads: 'Too much and too long, we seem to have surrendered community excellence and community values in the mere accumulation of material things. Our gross national product ... if we should judge America by that – counts air pollution and cigarette advertising, and ambulances to clear our highways of carnage. It counts special locks for our doors and the jails for those who break them. It counts the destruction of our redwoods and the loss of our natural wonder in chaotic sprawl. It counts napalm and the cost of a nuclear warhead, and armoured cars for police who fight riots in our streets. It counts Whitman's rifle and Speck's knife, and the television programs which glorify violence in order to sell toys to our children. Yet the gross national product does not allow for the health of our children, the quality of their education, or the joy of their play. It does not include the beauty of our poetry or the strength of our marriages; the intelligence of our public debate or the integrity of our public officials. It measures neither our wit nor our courage; neither our wisdom nor our learning; neither our compassion nor our devotion to our country; it measures everything, in short, except that which makes life worthwhile. And it tells us everything about America except why we are proud that we are Americans.'

5 UK Independence Party MEP Godfrey Bloom, quoted on www.bbc. co.uk, article dated 15 November 2012.

6 UN General Assembly Resolution of 19 July 2011, quoted on www. un.org.

7 'National Wellbeing Policy and a Weighted Approach to Human Feelings', Gus O'Donnell and Andrew J. Oswald, October 2015.

8 John Sloman, *Economics*, p. 1 (London: Harvester Wheatsheaf, 1991).

9 Data from 2012 UK ONS results *op. cit.* 'Married' includes people in Civil Partnerships, 'Cohabiting' includes same sex couples (but not in a Civil Partnership), 'Widowed' includes surviving civil partners and 'Divorced' includes people who are separated and separated/dissolved Civil Partnerships.

10 Professor Robert E. Lane, quoted in the *Miami Herald*, 28 May 2000.

11 Data from the 'World Values Survey' 1999–2002, analysed by The New Economics Foundation in 'The Happy Planet Index: an index of human wellbeing and environmental impact', 2006.

12 Disraeli, Benjamin, *Sybil, Or the Two Nations* (Oxford: Oxford University Press, 1998), quoted on www.victorianweb.org.

13 The relative poverty measure uses the median average, i.e. the income of the fiftieth percentile person. This is slightly lower than the mean average of all incomes, because the presence of a few ultra-high earners tends to pull the mean upwards.

14 A study looking at recipients of government handouts in rural Kenya concluded that their observed rise in happiness was exactly offset by a decline for those who did not receive the extra cash; and that both effects 'wore off' within a year. The impacts of additional wealth thus appeared to be entirely relational in nature, leading *The Economist* newspaper to conclude that 'money can buy you happiness – but only fleetingly, and at others' expense'. Quoted in *The Economist*, 31 October 2015.

15 Life satisfaction by nation shows a positive correlation with the Freedom House index of societal freedoms, and the World Bank 'voice and accountability index' which measures democracy and individual rights. This correlation remains strong even within developed (OECD) nations. New Economics Foundation, 'The Happy Planet Index' *op. cit.*

16 *The Bible*, Proverbs 20:14, New International Version.

17 Normally attributed to Ralph Waldo Emerson, 1803–1882, although it seems that the popular phrase is an adaptation of one of Emerson's sayings as the sprung mousetrap was not patented until several years after his death.

18 Robert F. Kennedy, *op. cit.*

19 ONS UK Labour Market statistical bulletin, August 2016, Figure 11 'UK Unemployment Rates 1971–2016'.

20 ONS 2012 *op. cit.* Fig. 4.1, 45% of unemployed respondents reported low or very low life satisfaction, compared to 20% of those in employment.

21 Obviously this is a considerable simplification. Price affects both supply and demand, and it will be different in both the short run (what price will enable me to sell everything I have today) and the long run (how many should I produce next month or year to maximise my profit?). For the unskilled labour market where the supply side is basically fixed by the number of people available for work, this simplification is reasonable and helpful to aid understanding.

22 The actual effects of introducing the UK minimum wage in 1999 and its subsequent increases in real terms have been slightly more complex than this. When it was first introduced, the loss of low-paid jobs predicted by some economists simply never happened. It seems that there are three main reasons for this. (1) The level of benefits paid to the unemployed was pretty much equal to the minimum wage, which meant that there was already little incentive for people to take the lowest-paid jobs. (2) The surplus of low-skilled workers put market power into the hands of employers, and probably meant that they were hiring staff for less than they would actually have been willing to pay (and turning the difference into profit). When this option was denied by the introduction of a minimum wage, excess profits were reduced but not eliminated so the jobs did not disappear. (3) Widespread non-compliance with the minimum wage in some industries such as catering and textiles. One example is where employers and workers collude to claim fraudulently that a job is part-time at minimum wage when it is actually full-time at less. The state conveniently makes up the difference with other low-income benefits, so everyone gains except the taxpayer. Professor David Metcalfe, 'On the Impact of the British National Minimum Wage on Pay and Employment', London School of Economics, 2006.

23 Of course there are numerous examples of unemployed people living fulfilled and active lives and making a great contribution to society. But sadly this is the exception rather than the norm. People in work show much higher levels of participation in voluntary and community activities, despite in theory having a lot less time on their hands to do so.

24 In 2015, the UK national minimum wage for workers over the age of 21 was £6.70 per hour – but the maths is complicated enough as it is without getting into fiddly fractions. The principle works for any level of

minimum wage, and it can be assumed that it will be adjusted annually in practice. It is also estimated that the minimum 'living wage' outside London is nearer £7.50 per hour, and in practice the difference is currently made up through in-work benefits. By managing the system to ensure that the new market pays at least the 'living wage', it would be possible to eliminate the need for most of these top-up payments which are complex and expensive to administer and vulnerable to fraud.

25 This obviously includes corporation tax, but given that the aim is to encourage uptake of the scheme it should also include PAYE, NI, capital gains, VAT, and any other taxation paid or collected by the employing business.

26 The adjustment would involve raising taxation by enough to cover the cost of tapered low-wage subsidies. This favours companies that employ large numbers of lower-paid workers over those that do not. Economists would suggest that this is a distortion of the free market and thus undesirable, but if we consider full employment to be a beneficial social outcome then manipulating the market to achieve it is a legitimate approach. Note that the current system uses corporate taxes to pay for unemployment, which is a distortion from which no companies benefit at all.

27 Economists suggest that there are two types of unemployment: 'frictional' (caused by the fact that it takes time to find and maybe train for a new job so some people will always be 'between jobs'), and 'structural' (a more fundamental problem that not enough jobs are available). The solution proposed in this chapter aims to sustainably eliminate structural unemployment without 'overheating' the rest of the economy. This still leaves the reality of frictional unemployment. Unemployment benefits to mitigate the impact of this on workers would need to be time-limited; e.g.: for a maximum number of weeks on each occasion and/or across a working lifetime. Interestingly, the UK system used to work in this way; time-limited benefits based on national insurance contributions paid while in work were significantly more generous than ongoing ones. However, the rise of seemingly permanent structural unemployment and associated means-tested long-term benefits means that there is now little different in practice for many people.

28 'My policy on cake is pro having it and pro eating it' was a favourite phrase of Boris Johnson MP, one of the leading figures in the 'Leave' campaign during the 2016 UK EU referendum.

29 The term 'social housing' in the UK includes property provided by local councils, housing associations, registered social landlords and 'arms-

lengths management organisations' (council owned but independently managed). For simplicity I use the terms interchangeably unless indicated to the contrary.

30 Market prices are median values for Thurrock local authority area taken from the government Local Housing Allowance website https://lha-direct.voa.gov.uk. Council rents are typical values for vacant properties as advertised in the local press, 2012.

31 The government at the time of writing is implementing a reduction of welfare payments for individuals who are 'under-occupying' larger homes to encourage them to down-size, but this obviously applies only to people living on welfare, not those in employment.

32 Following the banking crash that began in 2008 and the sovereign debt crisis which followed, even banks and government bonds are no longer regarded as entirely safe. In this case our hypothetical UK investor would be covered by the Financial Services Compensation Scheme (a government 'insurance of last resort') for the first £75,000 of deposits lost in any bank which went bust, so they should be OK.

33 The 'Local Housing Allowance', introduced in the UK in 2008 for welfare recipients renting private housing, adopts exactly this approach. LHA pays the thirtieth percentile local market rent for the appropriate property size based on assessed need, and from there the tenant is empowered to make their own choices. They can go cheaper and pocket the difference, or pay extra from their own resources if they wish. If the same principle is incorporated into the 'universal credit' reforms which started from 2013, then they would be compatible with these proposed changes with no further adjustment. https://lha-direct.voa.gov.uk.

34 A simple example: a housing association which moves to charging market rents for its properties will see a significant increase in the financial value of its housing assets. If it keeps this gain on its own balance sheet, the state will not have those resources available to fund the higher welfare payments that balance the system. The most obvious solution is a 100% 'windfall tax' on these one-off capital gains, which transfers the benefits of increased asset values back to the state which is funding them through the welfare system, while leaving the housing association in a financially neutral position. The state could close the loop by offering guaranteed loans to cover the same amount back to the housing associations, which achieves the required financial effect with minimal disruption. This approach has already been used successfully during the localisation of council housing assets to local authorities from central government in 2012/13.

35 There is a reasonable argument that the state should retain a stake in the property market for as long as it remains liable for paying the housing costs of welfare recipients. Otherwise it runs the risk that property prices and rents may rise (as has happened in the past) leaving it with greater outgoings but no corresponding additional sources of income. In modern financial markets it is possible to offset or 'hedge' this risk without physically owning bricks and mortar if desired. What matters is that the management of these properties merges into the normal operation of the housing market; something which state enterprises are not traditionally good at and which will involve changes even if the underlying asset ownership is retained.

36 Average UK house price: £162,900. Source: Land Registry, July 2012. Median UK gross annual earnings: £26,200. Source: Office for National Statistics 2011 income survey.

37 'Measuring National Well-being, Where we Live, 2012', Office for National Statistics. 32% of renters report low life satisfaction, compared with 20% of home owners. Correspondingly, 80% of homeowners report medium/high life satisfaction compared with just 68% of renters.

38 Cash value of average UK house in July 2012: £162,900 *op. cit.* Total repayments on a 6% mortgage for £162,900 over 25 years: £315,000. Source: www.moneyadviceservice.org.uk, mortgage calculator.

39 Summarised in *Seven Steps to Justice*, Rodney Shakespeare and Peter Challen (London: New European Publications, 2002). As a practical politician I still consider many of Shakespeare and Challen's ideas pretty implausible, but then as now I had to admit that they were definitely asking some important questions.

40 The biblical book of Job (chapter 28) gives an account of the mining, refining, and use of gold as a store of value which suggests that these practices were well established by the period 2000–1000 BC. Gold is portrayed in this chapter as distinctly inferior in value to wisdom, an observation that seems to have been largely forgotten by modern economics.

41 Paper bank notes can of course be lost, but that isn't the banks' problem because they don't create bank notes, they create loans and accept deposits back to finance them. Bank notes printed by the government become just one more transaction; you 'buy' them from the bank using money in your account when you withdraw cash, and 'sell' them back when you deposit it. In modern economies, cash money makes up just a few percent of the total in circulation.

42 The main international agreements governing capital ratios for banks are the Basel accords. Inevitably they are a lot more complex than this simple example suggests, giving different weightings to different types of assets included in the capital reserves.

43 'If you lend money to any of My people who are poor among you, you shall not be like a moneylender to him; you shall not charge him interest.' *The Bible*, Exodus 22:24, New King James Version.

44 Details from *The World Will Never Be The Same Again*, ed. Marlene Barrett (London: Jubilee 2000 Coalition and World Vision, 2000).

45 Economist and Jubilee Debt campaigner Ann Pettifor argues that the main proponents of ending the ban on charging interest in Christian Europe were John Eck and John Calvin, in the early to mid-1500s.

46 The surge recorded at the end of the England–Germany match on the evening of 4 July 1990 was 2800MW; enough to power an entire city of over 3 million people.

47 A central bank is the state-controlled institution which issues the currency and normally oversees and regulates the rest of the banking sector. Examples include the Bank of England, the US Federal Reserve, and the European Central Bank.

48 This assumes that the country issues its own currency. For nations which are part of a currency union such as the current Euro zone, such action would require agreement by the central bank and its collective rule makers.

49 All data from UN World Institute for Development Economics Research, 'The World Distribution of Household Wealth', February 2008.

50 Exactly what is meant by 'interest free' is a debate in itself. Investors consider the 'real rate of return' to be the percentage achieved above inflation. If inflation was running at 3%, it could be argued that a 3% loan is 'interest free' in real terms. Given that our objective in this case is at least partly redistributive, I am assuming that such loans would be interest free in absolute terms, with no percentages being levied at all. The only costs that would be added on would be a small administration charge. Although the money is created by the central bank, the actual mechanism for channelling it to borrowers would be through conventional retail lenders, who would compete on fees and quality of service for the business.

51 ONS 'Wellbeing, Where We Live', 2012, *op. cit.*

52 There are a number of reasons why it might be desirable to do something a bit more complex than simply base the maximum loan amount on national average property prices. One is regional price variation; the

'average house price' goes a lot further in Liverpool than in London (although further subsidising London purchasers would tend to perpetuate this divide). The other is the effect on couples and families. Larger households have genuinely greater housing needs and, as we will see in later chapters, couples already face a range of financial penalties. A poolable personal allowance of 50% of average house price per adult would allow a single person to buy a flat and a couple to acquire a house, without encouraging under-occupation for one-person households, which makes no contribution to wellbeing and unnecessarily increases the demand for larger properties.

53 In practice it might be desirable to limit this form of lending to, say, 95% or 98% of the property value, much as the banks already do. Taking on home ownership is a significant financial responsibility, and saving up for a deposit is a valuable form of preparation which can help prevent people falling into the misery of debt and repossession later on.

54 Repayments at 0% interest on an average loan of £162,900 over 25 years: £543 per month. Repayments on a commercial mortgage at 6% interest over the same duration: £1,050. Source: www.moneyadviceservice.org. uk.

55 Most bonds are actually issued for a fixed duration and repaid in full at the end. By adjusting the profile of long-term and short-term debt the government can effectively manage its repayment profile. If there are more bonds due to end their term in a given year than the nation wants or can afford to repay, it will re-borrow the money in a process known as 'rolling over the debt'.

56 As Chancellor of the Exchequer, former Prime Minister Gordon Brown articulated a 'golden rule' of public finances that the budget must balance across a full economic cycle. In other words, borrowing in lean times to maintain public spending is acceptable provided it is paid back during stronger times. Unfortunately what was thought to be a 'normal' economic growth cycle during the 2000s actually turned out to be a long credit-fuelled boom. When the spectacular bust came in 2008 the British government was already in significant debt and running a budget deficit, rather than being in surplus with a reserve fund to cover the subsequent downturn as the 'golden rule' would have demanded.

57 O'Donnell and Oswald, *op. cit.*

58 The London Borough of Barking and Dagenham is a traditionally white working-class area of east London. In the 2011 census, the proportion of ethnic White British residents dropped below 50% for the first time, and in some of the electoral wards of Barking itself the figure was below 25%.

59 *The Bible*, Revelation 7:9. The same combination of four characteristics used together to represent the full breadth of humanity occurs seven times, in 5:9, 7:9, 10:11, 11:9, 13:7, 14:6 and 17:15.

60 A 'genetic map' of the UK produced by researchers at Oxford University was one of the more controversial exhibits at the Royal Society 2012 summer exhibition; http://sse.royalsociety.org/2012/exhibits/genetic-maps/.

61 Racial divisions *within* America are a different issue. Clearly there is a lot of history between black and white in the USA, but we are talking here about national identity and it is interesting that neither group would normally challenge the other's American-ness on racial grounds. The picture has been made more complex by large numbers of often illegal immigrants from Mexico and Latin America, who are unable to integrate in the way that previous waves of migrants have done and thus lack the traditional markers of adopted American identity.

62 'Eastenders' is a long running British TV soap opera set in the east end of London. I am assuming that Shakespeare requires no explanation.

63 We could even come up with a mathematical formula for it: $D = 1 - \Sigma p^2$, where D is a diversity coefficient, and p is the proportion of the population made up by each of our defined diversity groups. So if the population was all made up of a single racial group (100% white British), D would be zero (not diverse at all). Thurrock in 2011 was in fact about 86% white British, 8% black, 4% Asian, and 2% other. Plug in the numbers and this gives a racial diversity of 0.25. You can use the same formula for other types of diversity too. Given that the population is split 50/50 between men and women, its gender diversity rather neatly works out at 0.5.

64 Although the diversity of society as a whole is largely fixed at a point in time, within individual organisations it does become possible to make proactive decisions about diversity. If an organisation is significantly different to the wider community in terms of its diversity characteristics, this may reveal a bias in recruitment or staff development practices which can then be addressed.

65 Citizenship Survey: 2010–11 (April 2010 – March 2011), England, Department for Communities and Local Government. Twenty-two percent of people thought that they would be treated worse than people of other races by at least one of the eight public service organisations measured.

66 This definition is the one currently adopted by the Crown Prosecution Service and Association of Chief Police Officers. The five monitored

strands (for which statistics are collected) are disability; race; religion or belief; sexual orientation; and transgender identity.

67 Thailand, although a democracy, is notorious for its '*lèse majesté*' laws which criminalise public criticism of the monarchy. In 2011, 60-year-old Ampon Tangnoppakul was jailed for 20 years for sending four text messages allegedly criticising the Thai royal family, and subsequently died in custody the following year.

68 *The Bible*, Luke 6:31.

69 The negative forms of the golden rule are 'don't do to others what you would not want done to you' or 'treat others as they treat you'. These both embody an element of reciprocity, but they lose the idea of an aspirational standard of behaviour and at worst can lead to a downwards spiral of revenge.

70 Data from UK Foreign Office website www.fco.gov.uk, country profile: Spain, updated 24 February 2012. '226k registered with the police and 1 million who spend at least part of the year in Spain'.

71 Article 'The other special relationship: the UAE and the UK' in *The National*, www.thenational.ae, 21 November 2010, gives a figure of 240,000 British citizens living in the UAE.

72 Current rules require ten years residence in Spain or to have been married to a Spanish national for at least one year.

73 According to UK census data, the foreign-born population of the UK grew from approximately 2 million (4%) to 7 million (11%) during the post-war period 1951 to 2011. The rate accelerated sharply during the final two decades, with absolute numbers doubling between 1991 and 2011.

74 The mechanisms for managing such a system are in fact already in place, because the processes for placing refugees and remunerating their hosts would be very similar to those used for providing foster care.

75 'Commissioning' is public sector jargon for providing a service by buying it in, usually from the private or community sector.

76 ONS, 'Wellbeing, Where We Live', 2012, *op. cit.*

77 All statistics in this section are taken from The Centre for Social Justice (CSJ) publications 'Breakdown Britain: Family Breakdown' (December 2006), 'Breakthrough Britain: Family Breakdown' (July 2007), and 'Family breakdown is not about divorce' (December 2010), unless otherwise cited.

78 'Children of the Great War', BBC News, www.bbc.co.uk 2007/11/09.

79 Department for Children, Schools, and Families, quoted on www.telegraph.co.uk, 16 November 2009.

80 ONS, 'Wellbeing, Where We Live', 2012, *op. cit.* 40% of divorced or separated people report 'low' or 'very low' life satisfaction, compared to around 30% for single or widowed people and 20% for couples.

81 Johnson (1991), quoted in CSJ 'Breakdown Britain' *op. cit.*

82 Two adults each earning £25,000 with no other factors to consider would pay £10,936 in combined income tax and national insurance. A single adult earning £50,000 and supporting a non-earning spouse would pay £14,221. Calculations for 2012/13 tax year using calculator at www. listentotaxman.com.

83 Case reported in the *Thurrock Yellow Advertiser*, 22 October 2009. The woman 'admitted four charges of claiming benefits fraudulently by failing to declare that her husband was living with her'.

84 Thurrock participates in the 'C-card' scheme, which enables young people under 25 to obtain free condoms at participating schools and pharmacies. Five different types of condoms are available, including ribbed 'pleasuremax' and flavoured versions. Children under the legal age of consent (16) are given six condoms per outlet per visit rather than 12. www.younghealth.co.uk/sex-relationships/c-card-scheme.

85 But not exclusively so. It is entirely possible to recognise alternative life choices as an outworking of personal and social freedom, without needing to degrade mainstream social norms in order to do so.

86 British scout troops now admit both boys and girls, but this was not yet the case when I served as a scout leader in my late teens.

87 The Royal Society for the Protection of Birds and the National Trust (along with smaller regional and local wildlife trusts) are nature and heritage charities which manage a national network of cultural, environmental, and leisure sites. Their membership has almost exactly mirrored the decline of political party membership, growing from a few hundred thousand to over 3 million today.

88 Citizenship Survey: 2010–11, *op. cit.* 25% of people reported that they volunteered formally at least once a month in 2010–11, a lower rate than at any point between 2001 and 2007–08 (when it ranged between 27% and 29%).

89 Churches in the UK still make up the single largest section of the voluntary and community sector. This also includes reference to other non-Christian faiths, although their contribution is still numerically smaller. Immigration has steadily increased the role played by Muslim, Hindu and Sikh faith groups in community activities, and has also further boosted the Christian contribution through the work of new 'black majority churches'.

90 In contrast to the 25% of the general population who volunteer (Citizenship Survey: 2010–11, *op. cit*), a 2011 survey by Christian Research and Evangelical Alliance showed that 81% of evangelical Christians are engaged in voluntary work at least once per month.

91 'Power of policy-making in the hands of philanthropists', www.bbc.co.uk/news/business-19272108, 2 September 2012.

92 Total giving to charities by UK adults 2010/11: £11 billion. Source: 'An overview of charitable giving in the UK, 2010/11', NCVO and CAF. Value of donations made through the 'gift aid' tax relief scheme in 2011, which allows charities to reclaim an additional 25% of basic-rate income tax paid by the donor: £3.8 billion. Source: The Halifax Giving Monitor, quoted on www.philanthropyuk.org, 28 June 2012.

93 Total government spending to charitable organisations in 2011 was £11.8 billion. Source: NCVO quoted on www.thirdsector.org.uk, 8 August 2011. This represents about 25% of total charity income, slightly exceeding in-year donations (other major sources include investment and endowment income and commercial activities). Given that not all of this goes to local, community-based initiatives, it can be seen that the total cost of a 100% community relief already sits within the current range of affordability. Total funding figures are, however, not the whole story, as far higher amounts are spent by government on services which could be delivered via the community but are currently provided through state or market means.

94 Shrove Tuesday occurs seven weeks before Easter. In the UK it is commonly known as 'pancake day', when sweet pancakes were traditionally eaten to mark the start of the Lenten fast.

95 As with all such rules of thumb, the reality is slightly more complicated, but these traditional definitions still hold true for a significant majority of locations.

96 The main option available beyond financial contributions is the imposition of planning conditions to mitigate particular negative aspects. An example might be to limit the hours of operation of a commercial site or require design and landscaping features on a housing estate.

97 The phrase NIMBYism is used to describe the phenomenon of local opposition to development ('Not In My Back Yard'). It is often portrayed as small minded, but in fact it reflects a reality that the positive benefits often apply at regional or even national level, while the more negative impacts are normally concentrated in the immediate locality. Hence people are rationally motivated to support the idea provided that it happens somewhere else.

98 In technical terms, the Euro zone is a monetary union (where countries share the same currency) but not a fiscal union (where they would share economic policies like levels of taxation and public spending).

99 A nation state with its own currency can experience a sovereign debt crisis, exchange rate fluctuations, and inflation, but these will then interact together as the resolution plays out. Nations in a currency union such as the Euro zone can experience a sovereign debt crisis without the ability to either devalue or inflate their currency as part of the resolution, leaving them with few options but to crash out or seek help from their currency partners.

100 Source: World Bank, data.worldbank.org, 2015.

101 And the less commonly used but still preserved Gaelic and Cornish languages.

102 In practice there are still some carbon emissions associated with mechanised agriculture, processing the oil, and transporting it to its destination. But even after these are taken into account, vegetable oil still contributes maybe 80% less to global warming than its fossil fuel equivalent.

103 Drivers do pay some additional taxes, including fuel duty and a vehicle licence fee. How far this goes towards paying the total social costs of car use including all the externalities is the subject of considerable debate.

104 Of course some people avoid driving at peak times because they have no particular need to do so. For them, the benefits of waiting are personal and make sense without even considering externalities. The real issue is the 10,000 drivers who, if they all took the train instead, could eliminate peak time congestion altogether. For them, the costs would be personal (a slightly more expensive and inconvenient trip to work) while the benefits go to someone else (those drivers who never made the switch and now enjoy clear roads as a result). This is actually an example of a 'positive externality'. By taking the train I create a social benefit in that the roads are clearer for everyone else. But just as I am not penalised for negative externalities, I also receive no personal reward for positive ones. This means that I have no incentive to create them (and so probably won't bother).

105 New Economics Foundation 2006, *op. cit.*, citing World Bank governance indicators.

106 The Icelandic case study is quoted from *Overfishing: The Icelandic Solution*, Prof. Hannes H. Gissurarson (London: Institute of Economic Affairs, 2000).

107 Like all predictive science, there is a significant degree of debate and controversy surrounding the extent and likely effects of man-made global warming. This is not a discussion I intend to get into here; the clear majority of opinion currently suggests that the effects are real enough and serious enough to make reducing carbon emissions an essential precaution for humanity to take.

108 At present there is no way of eliminating carbon dioxide emissions from fossil fuels, so it can be assumed that all the carbon in the fuel will eventually end up as CO_2. Emerging technologies such as carbon capture and storage may change this position in the future, but given that they are only likely to work on massive industrial scales it will be fairly easy to identify the benefits and offer appropriate discounts.

109 Provisional UK tax revenues in 2010/11 were £541 billion. In 2011/12, each 1% of basic rate UK income tax was worth £4.75 billion, each 1% of higher rate income tax £0.78 billion, and each 1% of corporation tax £0.75 billion. On this basis, £50 billion would fund an eight-point reduction in income and corporation tax. However, this still represents less than 10% of overall tax take. It all depends on which taxes and bands are reduced, but a headline cut of at least a third in the most obvious direct taxes (income and corporation tax) is entirely feasible. Source: http://www.parliament.uk/business/publications/research/key-issues-for-the-new-parliament/the-public-finances/structure-of-taxation/

110 The aim is to reduce scheme emissions by 20% by 2020 compared to 1990 levels, to support commitments made under the Kyoto protocol. The first few years of the scheme did not demand significant reductions in emissions, but focused primarily on getting the market for permits established.